## Introduction



## A: Legal and management



## B: Health and welfare



## C: General safety



## D: High risk activities



## E: Environment

## F: Specialist activities

If you are preparing for a specialist test you also need to revise the appropriate specialist activity, from those listed below.



## Further information

# Introduction

**Contents**

# Foreword

In the construction industry we are all responsible for the health and safety of ourselves and of those who work around us. You might ask, 'Why is this – surely I can't be expected to look after others I don't even know?' It's not just the law that demands we care for ourselves and those around us. Even if you are not responsible for setting people to work on site, you still have a moral duty to look out for each other. In other words, it's the right thing to do.

Think about it: you might be the most experienced person on site, or the person most familiar with the job. Maybe you've tackled this work many times before and know the safest method, while others around you might not have a clue. As an experienced worker, you have a voice and you can speak up to help make the job safer. Then again, you might be new to construction and still finding your feet.

Both experienced and new workers have a duty to care for the health, safety and wellbeing of themselves and others working on site, and both need the right knowledge to do that. CITB revision material helps give you this knowledge, whether you are doing the job for the first or the hundredth time.

Construction is still one of the country's most dangerous industries. Each year around 80,000 workers suffer an illness that they believe was caused or made worse by their work. Around 52,000 of these are cases of bad backs, damaged shoulders or similar injuries, 12,000 are due to stress, anxiety and depression and 3,000 are from breathing and lung problems. Although the fatal accident figures have generally improved over the last twenty years, construction workers are still dying from work-related causes. We can all agree that even one death is one too many.

CITB is committed to equipping those who step onto Great Britain's construction sites with the appropriate knowledge and skills. Our *Health, safety and environment test* is designed to give you the right knowledge so that you can spot dangers on site and confidently take steps to stop problems from happening. The test is continuously reviewed to ensure it is fit for purpose, and some new question styles are being introduced in 2018.

We all want to make sites safe places where no-one's health is harmed. CITB is here to help you do that. Working together, looking out for each other, we can raise health and safety standards and make a positive impact on our industry.

Revd. Eur Ing Kevin Fear BSc (Hons), CEng, MICE, CMIHT, CMIOSH, Hon FaPS
Health and Safety Strategy Lead
CITB

# About this book

This book has been created to help you revise for your *Health, safety and environment test*. It contains all of the questions that you may be presented with when you take your test. It also includes information about how to book your test, any special assistance that is available and other helpful topics.

To help you get the most from the book, it has been designed for you to use as a workbook. You can test yourself by marking your answers in the book and then checking these against the correct answers at the back of the book.

# About the test

The CITB *Health, safety and environment test* helps raise standards across the industry. It ensures that workers meet a minimum level of health, safety and environmental awareness before going on site.

The test structure has been designed to enable you to demonstrate knowledge across the following key areas.

**Section A: Legal and management**

**Section B: Health and welfare**

**Section C: General safety**

**Section D: High risk activities**

**Section E: Environment**

**Section F: Specialist activities**

### Section A: Legal and management

**General responsibilities:** what you and your employer need to do to ensure everyone is working safely on site.

**Accident reporting and recording:** when, how and why accidents need to be reported and recorded.

### Section B: Health and welfare

**Health and welfare:** common health issues on site and how to avoid them. Providing welfare facilities and support on site.

**First aid and emergency procedures:** what you should do in case of an emergency, and what your employer must make available.

**Personal protective equipment:** why personal protective equipment (PPE) is important, why you should wear it and who is responsible for it.

**Dust and fumes (Respiratory hazards):** how to work safely, protecting yourself and those around you from exposure to respiratory hazards. What health conditions may arise from exposure to dust and fumes.

**Noise and vibration:** why it is important to minimise exposure to noise and vibration in the workplace. How you should protect yourself and those around you.

**Hazardous substances:** how you can identify a hazardous substance, and what control measures should be in place to enable you to work safely.

**Manual handling:** why and how it is important to handle all loads using a safe system of work. What key areas you need to be aware of when handling loads.

### Section C: General safety

**Safety signs:** what type of safety signs you will see on a construction site, and what they are informing you of.

**Fire prevention and control:** what you should do if you discover a fire, and which fire extinguishers should be used on what type of fire.

**Electrical safety, tools and equipment:** how to work safely with different types of tools, and what you should do if the tools you are using have not been examined or are faulty.

**Site transport safety and lifting operations:** how careful planning can safely segregate pedestrian and traffic routes, traffic rules you need to be aware of, and how to lift loads safely.

### Section D: High risk activities

**Working at height:** what types of equipment you will use for working at height, and how to use them correctly.

**Excavations and confined spaces:** how to work safely in a confined space or excavation, and what you should do if exposed to certain hazards.

### Section E: Environment

**Environmental awareness and waste control:** your responsibilities on site, how waste should be managed and how to conserve energy.

### Section F: Specialist activities

If you are preparing for a specialist test you will also be asked questions about your specialist activity. There are currently 12 specialist tests available, including supervisory; demolition; highway works; specialist work at height; lifts and escalators; tunnelling; plumbing (JIB); heating and plumbing services; pipefitting and welding; ductwork; refrigeration and air conditioning; services and facilities maintenance.

## How is the test structured?

All tests last for 45 minutes and have 50 questions. Tests are made up of behavioural case study questions and knowledge questions.

## What is a behavioural case study question?

The behavioural case study questions are designed to test how you respond to health and safety situations on a construction site.

Three case studies are included at the beginning of your test, each of which has four linked multiple-choice questions.

The questions progress through a fictional situation faced by an individual working in the construction industry. They are based on the principles established in the film *Setting out* – what you should expect from a site and what they expect from you.

Further information on the film and the transcript is provided at the back of this book.

## What is a knowledge question?

The knowledge questions cover 16 core areas (presented in Sections A–E of this book) that are included in all the tests. These questions are factual. For example, they will ask you to identify fire extinguishers and signs. There is an additional knowledge question bank for each specialist test.

You do not need to have a detailed knowledge of the exact content of any regulations. However, you do need to show that you know what is required of you, the things you must do (or not do), and what to do in certain circumstances (for example, upon discovering an accident).

Legislation in Northern Ireland and Scotland differs from that in the rest of the UK. For practical reasons, all candidates (including those in Northern Ireland and Scotland) will be tested on questions using legislation relevant to the remainder of the UK only.

There are six different styles of knowledge question that may be presented within your test. These are explained below.

### Multiple choice and multiple choice with images

**Multiple-choice questions are identified by this icon.**

A multiple-choice question will ask you to select one or more answers from a list of options. Some answer options may also contain images.

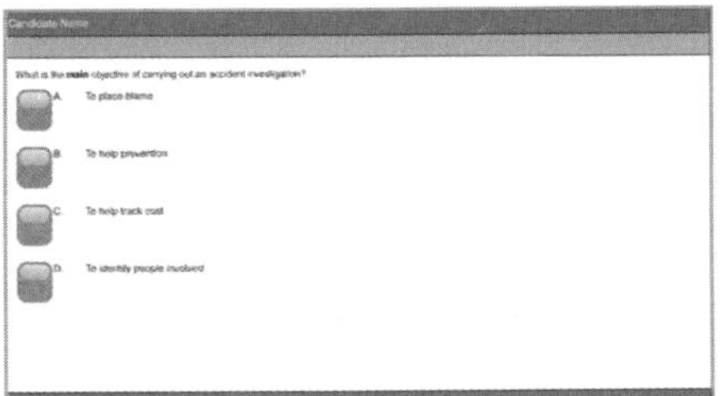

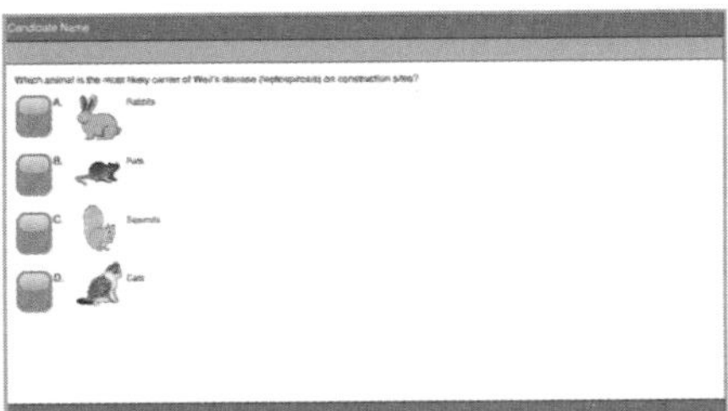

### Drag and drop text and drag and drop images

**Drag and drop questions are identified by this icon.**

A drag and drop question can be answered by dragging and dropping text or images from a list of options to the answer area.

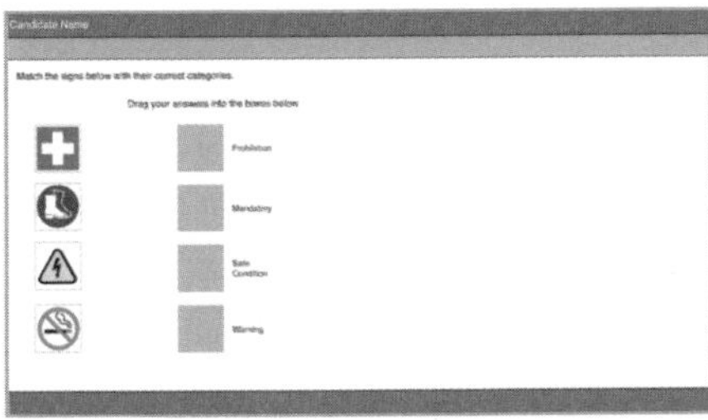

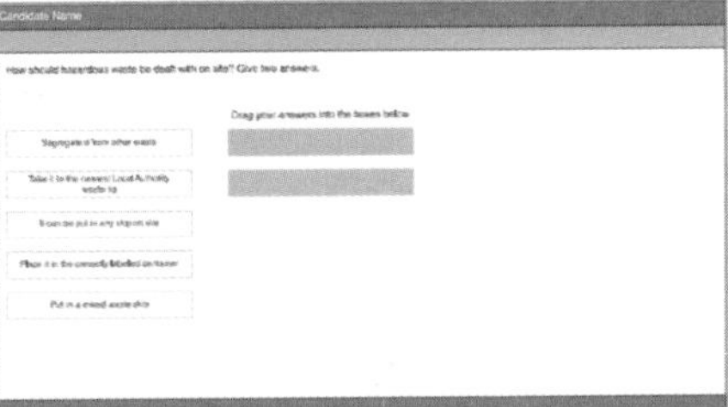

### Hot spot

**Hot spot questions are identified by this icon.**

A hot spot question can be answered by selecting the correct place on the given image.

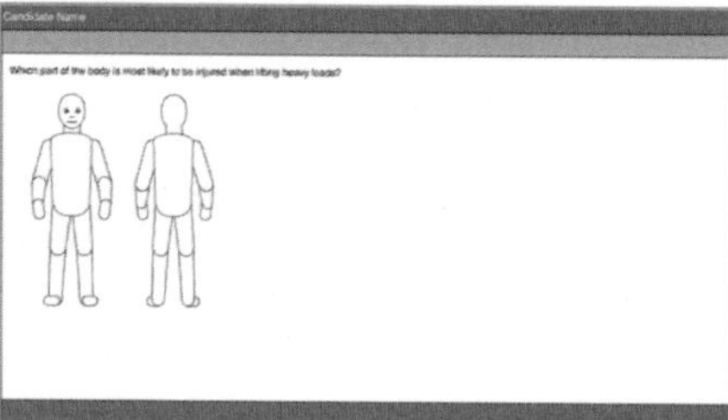

### Hot area

**Hot area questions are identified by this icon.**

A hot area question can be answered by selecting one of the answer areas within the given image.

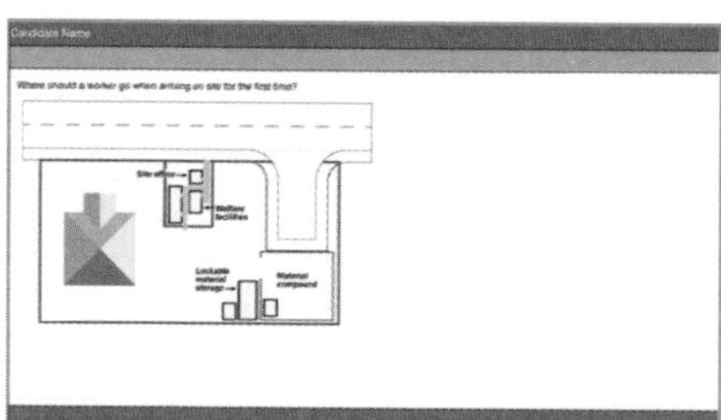

 To practise these question styles online, visit www.citb.co.uk/hsandetest

## Who writes the questions?

The question bank is developed by CITB with industry-recognised organisations which sit on or support the health, safety and environment test question sub-committee. A full list of those parties that support the test is set out in the acknowledgements at the back of this book.

## Will the questions change?

Health, safety and environment legislation, regulations and best practice will change from time to time, but CITB makes every effort to keep the test and the revision material up to date.

- You will not be tested on questions that are deemed to be no longer current.
- You will be tested on knowledge questions presented in the most up-to-date edition of the book. To revise effectively for the test you should use the latest edition. You can check which edition of the book you have at www.citb.co.uk/hsandetest or phone 0344 994 4488.

The *Health, safety and environment test* is currently under development. To find further information about the development taking place and how this affects you, visit www.citb.co.uk/hsandetest

# Preparing for a test

To pass your *Health, safety and environment test* you need to demonstrate knowledge and understanding across a number of areas, all of which are relevant to people working in a construction environment. There is not a minimum pass mark but sectional scoring, with minimum scores allocated to each section. This test structure has been designed to enable you to demonstrate knowledge across all of these key areas.

There are a number of ways you can prepare for your test and increase your success.

| Revision material | Operatives | Specialists | Supervisors | Managers |
|---|---|---|---|---|
| Watch *Setting out* | To help prepare for the behavioral case studies, watch the free to view video *Setting out* at www.citb.co.uk/settingout | | | |
| Read the question and answer books | *HS&E test for operatives and specialists* (GT 100) | | | *HS&E test for managers and professionals* – (GT 200) |
| Use the digital products | *HS&E test for operatives and specialists*<br>– DVD (GT 100 DVD)<br>– Download (GT 100 DL)<br>– App<br>Take a simulated test<br>*Safe start* (GE 707 DL) | | | *HS&E test for managers and professionals*<br>– DVD (GT 200 DVD)<br>– Download (GT 200 DL)<br>– App |
| Read supporting knowledge material | *Safe start* (GE 707) | *Safe start* (GE 707) plus sector recommended supporting material | *Site supervision simplified* (GE 706) | *Construction site safety* (GE 700) |
| Complete an appropriate training course | Site Safety Plus – one-day *Health and safety awareness* course | Contact your industry body for recommendations | Site Safety Plus – two-day *Site supervision safety training scheme* | Site Safety Plus – five-day *Site management safety training scheme* |

## Where can I buy additional revision material?

CITB has developed a range of revision material, including question and answer books, DVDs, downloads and a smartphone app that will help you to prepare for the test. For further information and to buy these products:

 go online at www.citb.co.uk/hsanderevision

 telephone 0344 994 4488

 visit the highstreet or online for books and DVDs. Visit the Apple App store or the Google Play store for smartphone apps.

 For further products and services that CITB offers visit citb.co.uk

## What's on the DVD, app and download?

The DVD, app and download offer an interactive package that includes:

- ☑ the *Setting out* film and a sample behavioural case study
- ☑ all the knowledge questions and answers in both book and practice format
- ☑ a test simulator – all the functionality of the test with the real question bank
- ☑ voice-overs in English and Welsh for all questions.

The DVD and app also provide operative questions and *Setting out* with voice-overs in 14 different languages.

Please note: British Sign Language assistance is included on the GT 100 revision DVD and within the *Setting out* film.

# Booking a test

The easiest way to book your test is either online or by telephone. You should be able to book a test at your preferred location within two weeks. You will be given the date and time of your test immediately and offered the opportunity to buy revision material (for example, a book, DVD, download or app).

To book your test:

 go online at www.citb.co.uk/hsandetest

 telephone 0344 994 4488
Welsh booking line 0344 994 4490

 post in an application form (application forms are available from the website and the telephone numbers listed above).

When booking your test you will be able to choose whether to receive confirmation by email or by letter. It is important that you check the details (including the type of test, the location, the date and time) and follow any instructions given regarding the test.

If you do not receive a confirmation email or letter within the time specified, please call the booking line to check your booking has been made.

## What information do I need to book a test?

To book a test you should have the following information to hand.

- Which test you need to take.
- Whether you require any special assistance (see below).
- Your chosen method of payment (debit or credit card details).
- Your personal details.
- Your CITB registration number, if you have taken a *Health, safety and environment test* before or applied for certain card schemes.

## What special assistance is available when taking the test?

### Voice-over assistance

All tests can be booked with English or Welsh voice-overs.

### Foreign language assistance

- The test for operatives can be booked with voice-overs in the following languages: Bulgarian, Czech, French, German, Hungarian, Lithuanian, Polish, Portuguese, Punjabi, Romanian, Russian and Spanish.

  An interpreter can be requested if assistance is required in other languages.
- The test for specialists can be booked with an interpreter but no pre-recorded voice-overs are available.

### Sign language assistance

The test for operatives can be booked with British Sign Language on screen. If you need assistance in the other tests a signer can be provided.

### Further assistance

If you need any other special assistance (such as a reader, signer, interpreter or extra time) this can be provided but you will need to book your test through a dedicated booking line: 0344 994 4491.

## How do I cancel or reschedule my test?

To cancel or reschedule your test you should go online or call the booking number at least 72 hours (three working days) before your test. There will be no charge for cancelling or rescheduling the test online at www.citb.co.uk/hsandetest outside of the 72-hour period. Reschedules and cancellations made via the telephone booking line will incur an administration fee.

# Taking a test

### On the day of the test you will need to:

- allow plenty of time to get to the test centre and arrive at least 15 minutes before the start of the test
- take your confirmation email or letter
- take proof of identity that includes your photo and your signature (such as a driving licence card or passport – please visit www.citb.co.uk/hsandetest for a full list of acceptable documentation).

On arrival at the test centre, staff will check your documents to ensure you are booked onto the correct test. If you do not have all the relevant documents you will not be able to sit your test and you will lose your fee.

### During the test

The tests are all delivered on a computer screen. However, you do not need to be familiar with computers and the test does not involve any typing. All you need to do is select the relevant answer(s), using either a mouse or by touching the screen.

Before the test begins you will work through a tutorial. It explains how the test works and lets you try out the buttons and functions that you will use while taking your test.

There will be information displayed on the screen which shows you how far you are through the test and how much time you have remaining.

### After the test

At the end of the test there is an optional survey that gives you the chance to provide feedback on the test process.

You will be provided with a printed score report after you have left the test room. This will tell you whether you have passed or failed your test, and give feedback on areas where further learning and revision are recommended.

## What do I do if I fail?

If you fail your test, your score report will provide you with information on the areas where you got questions wrong.

It is strongly recommended that you revise these areas thoroughly before re-booking. You will have to wait at least 48 hours before you can take the test again.

If you require a detailed score report showing the questions you were asked, the answers you gave and the correct answers, please email testingservicesfeedback@citb.co.uk

## What do I do if I pass?

Once you have passed your test, you should consider applying to join the relevant card scheme, if you have not done so already. However, please be aware that you may need to complete further training, assessment and/or testing to meet their specific entry requirements.

To find out more about many of the recognised schemes:

 go online at www.citb.co.uk/cards-testing/

## Fraudulent testing

If you are aware of any fraudulent activity in the delivery of your test, or relating to cards or training in the construction industry:

 email our fraud investigation team at report.it@citb.co.uk

CITB takes reports of fraud linked to our testing processes extremely seriously. Working with the Police and other law enforcement agencies, we are doing everything we can to address the issue. Where possible, we always prosecute those engaged in any fraudulent activity.

# Augmented reality

## What is augmented reality?

Augmented reality (AR) technology is used in this revision book to provide readers with additional digital content such as videos, images and weblinks.

This technology has been used to connect you with extra content, free of charge. It can be accessed via your mobile device using the Layar app.

### How to install and use the Layar app

- ☑ Go to the appropriate app store (Apple or Android) and download the Layar app (free of charge) to your mobile device.
- ☑ Look out for the AR logo (right), which indicates a Layar-friendly page or image.

- ☑ Open the Layar app and scan the Layar-friendly page or image (ensure that you have the whole page or the specific image in view whilst scanning).
- ☑ Wait for the page to activate on your device.
- ☑ Select one of the buttons, when they appear, to access the additional content.

## Where can I find augmented reality in this revision book?

The following content is accessible by scanning the cover page of this publication.

- ☑ Book a *Health, safety and environment test*.
- ☑ Watch the *Setting out* film.
- ☑ Buy additional revision material.

# A
# Legal and management

## Contents

A
01

# 01 General responsibilities

**1.01** Who is responsible for reporting any unsafe conditions on site?

A The client

B Site manager

C The contracts manager

• D Everyone on site

**1.02** During site induction you do not understand something the presenter says. What should you do?

A Attend another site induction

• B Ask the presenter to explain it again

C Guess what the presenter was saying

D Wait until the end then ask someone else to explain

**1.03** What should you do if the safety rules given in your site induction seem out of date as work progresses?

A Nothing, as safety is the site manager's responsibility

• B Speak to your supervisor about your concerns

C Speak to your workmates to see if they have any new rules

D Make up your own safety rules to suit the changing conditions

**1.04** What is the **most** important reason for keeping your work area clean and tidy?

• A To help prevent slips, trips and falls

B It saves time cleaning up at the end of the week

C So that waste skips can be emptied more often

D To recycle waste and help the environment

**1.05** Who should you speak to if the work of another contractor is affecting your safety?

A Your workmates

• B Your supervisor

C The contractor's supervisor

D The contractor who is doing the job

A 01

**1.06** Where should a worker go when arriving on site for the **first** time?

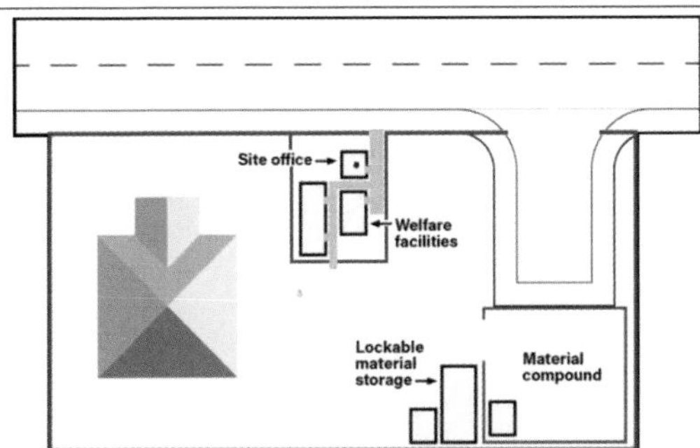


**1.07** What does it mean if the equipment you are using is issued with a prohibition notice?

A You must not use it unless your supervisor is present

B You must not use it until it is made safe

C You can use it as long as you take more care

D Only supervisors can use it until further notice

**1.09** The whole site has been issued with a prohibition notice. What does this mean?

A Continue with site work

B Do not use any power tools

C Finish the job and go home

D Stop work because the site is unsafe

**1.08** Why is the Health and Safety at Work etc. Act important to you as a worker? Give **two** answers.

Drag your answers into the boxes below

A It states how to make legal claims after an accident

B It tells employers who is working where on site

C It puts legal duties on all employers

D It states how employees should carry out a task

E It puts legal duties on all employees

A
01

**1.10** After watching you work, a Health and Safety Executive (HSE) inspector issues an improvement notice. What does this mean?

A You are not working fast enough

B You need to improve the standard of your work

• C You are not working in a safe way

D Your work has improved since the last visit

**1.13** Who has legal duties under the Health and Safety at Work etc. Act?

A Employers only

B Employees only

• C All people at work

D Only self-employed people

**1.11** State **two** reasons why the Health and Safety at Work etc. Act 1974 is important to construction employers?

Drag your answers into the boxes below

A It states how to make legal claims after an accident

B It tells employers who is working on site

C • It puts legal duties on all employers

D It lets workers know how to carry out a task

E • It puts legal duties on all employees

**1.12** Which of these is your legal duty as a worker?

A To continue to work until all tasks are completed

B To write method statements for site tasks

• C To report anything thought to be dangerous

D To write risk assessments for site tasks

**1.14** Who is responsible for managing health and safety on site?

A Building inspector

B Contracts manager

C Health and Safety Executive (HSE)

• D Site manager

**1.15** What does a risk assessment identify?

A How to report accidents

B The site working hours

C The hazards in the work environment

D Where the first-aid kit is kept

**1.16** What does the word **hazard** mean?

A Anything that could cause harm to people

B The construction site accident rate

C A type of removable barrier or machine guard

D The likelihood of something happening

**1.18** You are about to start a job. How will you know if it needs a permit to work?

A Other workers on site will pass them on after they have finished with them

B The Health and Safety Executive (HSE) will give them out

C Information will be given during the site induction before any work starts

D Permits to work are only required by managers on large sites

**1.19** What should you do if you cannot do a job in the way described in the method statement?

A Make up a better way to do it and carry on

B Do not start work until you have talked to your supervisor

C Ask other workers how they think it should be done

D Contact the Health and Safety Executive (HSE)

**1.17** Which **two** topics should be covered in a site induction?

Drag your answers into the boxes below

A Site rules

B Local transportation links

C Holiday entitlement

D Site emergency procedures

E Local amenities

**1.20** What does a permit to work allow?

A The emergency services to come on to the site after an accident

• B Tasks to be carried out safely under strictly controlled conditions

C Health and Safety Executive (HSE) inspectors to visit the site without warning

D Untrained people to operate certain tools without supervision

**1.21** How would you expect to find out about site health and safety rules when you **first** arrive on site?

• A During site induction

B In a letter sent to your home

C By reading your employer's health and safety policy

D By asking other workers on the site to show you around

**1.23** Why is it your employer's legal responsibility to discuss matters of health and safety with you?

A So that you will never have to attend any other health and safety training

B So that your employer will not have any legal responsibility for your health and safety

• C So that you are informed of things that will protect your health and safety

D So you do not have any responsibilities for health and safety

**1.24** What is a toolbox talk?

• A A short training session on a particular safety topic

B A talk that tells you where to buy tools

C Your first training session when you arrive on site

D A sales talk given by a tool supplier

**1.22** What are **two** possible consequences for employers of **not** taking measures to prevent accidents and ill health at work?

Drag your answers into the boxes below

• A They could be fined or imprisoned

B They will have to change the site layout for emergency vehicles

• C They will lose time and money due to the cost of any accident or ill health

D They will need to employ more people

E They will damage the environment

**1.25** What is the **main** reason for attending a site induction?

A To get to know other new employees on site

B To create the method statements for the site

C Site health and safety rules and site hazards will be explained

D Permits to work will be written and handed out

**1.26** What are **two** possible consequences for you if your employer does **not** prevent accidents and ill health at work?

A You will have to work longer hours to earn the same income

B You may suffer an injury, affecting your health and wellbeing

C You won't get the training required to continue working on site

D You may not be able to work, which would affect your income and family life

E You will have worse welfare facilities on site while improvements are made

A 02

# 02 Accident reporting and recording

**2.01** Which **two** of the following will help you to find out about the site emergency procedures and emergency telephone numbers?

- A Guidance from the Health and Safety Executive (HSE) website
- B Reading the site noticeboards
- C Guidance from your local job centre
- D Attending the site induction
- E Looking in the telephone directory

**2.04** What should be done in the event of an emergency on site?

- A Leave site by the nearest exit and return home
- B Collect your personal items and leave site
- C Follow the site emergency procedure
- D Phone the Health and Safety Executive (HSE) for advice

**2.02** What **two** things should you do if there is an emergency situation on site?

Drag your answers into the boxes below

- A Go to the designated assembly point
- B Look for other people who may not know what to do
- C Finish what you are doing
- D Collect personal items from the site office
- E Leave the area via the nearest exit

**2.03** You have witnessed a serious accident on your site and are to be interviewed by a Health and Safety Executive (HSE) inspector. What should you do?

- A Ask your supervisor what you should tell the inspector
- B Not tell the inspector anything, and ask them to talk to your supervisor
- C Co-operate and tell the inspector exactly what you saw
- D Ask other workers what you should tell the inspector

**2.05** What is the main objective of carrying out an accident investigation?

- A To place blame
- B To find out the cause to prevent it happening again
- C To help track cost
- D To identify people involved

**2.06** A scaffold has collapsed and you saw it happen. What should you say when you are asked about the accident?

A As little as possible, as you are not a scaffold expert

B As little as possible because you don't want to get people into trouble

C Exactly what you saw, giving as much detail as possible

D Who you think should be blamed and punished

**2.07** When **must** accidents be recorded in the accident book?

A If a person is injured in any way

B Only if a person suffers a broken bone

C If a person has a day off work with a cold

D Only if a person has to attend hospital

**2.08** If someone is injured at work, who should record it in the accident book?

A The company contract manager

B The injured person or someone acting for them

C The first aider identified on site

D Someone from the Health and Safety Executive (HSE)

**2.09** Which of these does **not** have to be recorded in the accident book?

A National insurance number

B The date and the time

C Details of the injury

D Your home address

**2.10** Which type of accidents should be recorded in the accident book?

A Specified injuries only, such as broken bones or a death

B Any injuries requiring treatment in a hospital

C All accidents causing any kind of injury

D Only accidents where time off work is required

**2.11** When **must** an accident be recorded?

A Only when an accident causes injury to a worker as a result of working activities

B Only when a person is injured and will be off work for three days or more

C Only when an accident causes damage to plant or equipment

D Only when a person breaks a major bone or is concussed

A 02

**2.12** Which **two** of the following items should be recorded in the accident book?

Drag your answers into the boxes below

- A National insurance number
- • B Date of the accident
- C Location of the hospital
- • D Injuries sustained
- E Telephone number

**2.13** When **must** an entry be made in the accident book?

- • A When an accident causes personal injury to any worker
- B When the person has been off sick for three days
- C When a compensation claim is made
- D When management thinks it appropriate

**2.14** You suffer an injury at work and the details are recorded into the accident book. What **must** happen to this accident record?

- A It must be sent to the insurance company at the end of the job
- B It must be kept in a place where anyone at work can read it
- • C It must be treated as confidential under the Data Protection Act
- D It must be destroyed at the end of the job, due to confidentiality

**2.15** Where should accidents that cause any injury be recorded?

- A In the main contractor's diary
- • B In the accident report book
- C In the site engineer's day book
- D In the building inspector's diary

**2.16** Which of the following is the **least** important reason for recording all accidents?

- A It might stop them happening again
- B Some types of accident have to be reported to the Health and Safety Executive (HSE)
- C Details have to be entered in the accident book
- • D To find out who is to blame and make sure they are prosecuted

**2.17** Why is it important to report near miss incidents on site?

- A It is the law to report all near miss incidents
- B To find someone to blame so claims can be made
- C It is a requirement of the CDM Regulations
- • D To learn from them and stop them happening again

**2.18** If you have a minor accident, who should report it?

- A Anyone who saw the accident
- B The sub-contractor
- • C You, if possible
- D The Health and Safety Executive (HSE)

**2.19** If your doctor says that you contracted Weil's disease (leptospirosis) on site, why do you need to tell your employer?

- A Your employer has to warn your colleagues not to go near you
- • B It must be reported to the Health and Safety Executive (HSE)
- C Your employer will need to call pest control to remove rats on site
- D The site on which you contracted it will have to be closed down

**2.20** While working on site you get a small cut on one of your fingers. What should you do?

- A Report it at the end of the day or the end of the shift
- B Wash it, and if it is not a problem carry on working
- C Clean it and tell your supervisor about it later
- • D Report it and get first aid if necessary

**2.21** You receive an injury from an accident at work. When should you report it?

- A At the end of the day, before you go home
- B Only if you have to take time off work
- • C Immediately, or as soon as possible
- D The next day before you start work

**2.22** Why should you report an accident?

- A It helps the site find out who caused it
- • B It is a legal requirement
- C So that everyone can find out what happened
- D So that your company will be held responsible

A 02

**2.23** You have been injured by an accident at work and, as a result, are absent for more than seven days. Which **two** of the following actions **must** be taken?

Drag your answers into the boxes below

- A The accident must be recorded in the accident book
- B The emergency services must be called to find out how the accident happened
- C The local hospital and the benefits office must be informed
- D Your employer must inform the Health and Safety Executive (HSE)
- E You must pay for any first-aid equipment used to treat your injury

**2.24** Who **must** you report a serious accident to?

- A Site security
- B The police service
- C Your employer
- D The ambulance service

**2.25** What should you do if you have witnessed a serious accident on your site?

- A Say nothing in case you get someone into trouble
- B Ask your workmates what they think you should do
- C Telephone the local doctor for advice
- D Tell your supervisor that you saw what happened

**2.26** Your doctor tells you that you have hand-arm vibration syndrome possibly caused through work. What should you do?

- A Tell no-one as it's not contagious
- B Inform your site supervisor or employer
- C Only inform your friends at work
- D Tell no-one as this is not reportable

**2.27** Which of the following statements **best** describes a near miss?

- A An incident where you were just too late to see what happened
- B An incident that nearly resulted in injury or damage
- C An incident where someone was injured and nearly had to go to hospital
- D An incident where someone was injured and nearly had to take time off work

# B

# Health and welfare

## Contents

# 03 Health and welfare



**3.01** What sort of rest area should your employer provide on site?

A A canteen serving food, drink and cold sandwiches

B A covered area with some comfortable chairs and running water

C A covered area, chairs, and a way to boil water and heat food

D Employers don't have to provide rest areas, as long as rest breaks are provided

**3.02** What are the legal **minimum** facilities that should be provided on site for washing your hands?

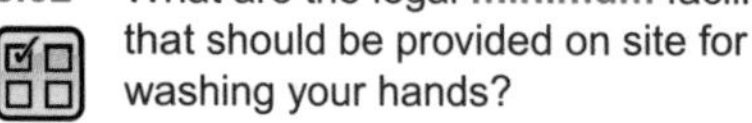

A There is no need to provide washing facilities

B A water container, bowl and paper towels

C A cold water standpipe and paper towels

D Hot and cold water, soap, and a way to dry your hands

**3.03** Where should you go on site to eat and drink?

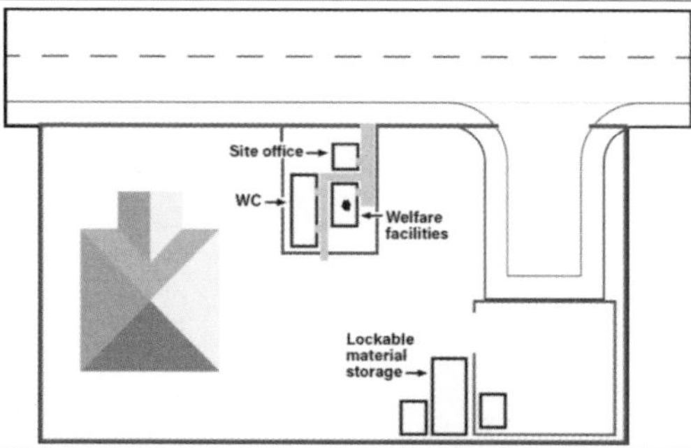


**3.04** If the toilets on your site are always dirty or do not flush, what should you do?

A Try not to use the toilets while you are at work

B Tell the person in charge of the site about the problem

C Try to fix the faulty toilet yourself

D See if you can use public toilets nearby

**3.05** What should you do if there is nowhere on site to wash your hands?

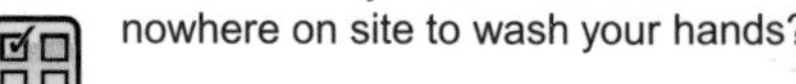

A Wait until you get home, then wash them

B Go to the local public toilets and use their washbasin

C Speak to your supervisor or the site manager about the problem

D Nothing, as the site does not have to provide washing facilities

**3.06** What are **two** ways of reducing the risk of transferring hazardous substances from your hands to your mouth?

Drag your answers into the boxes below

- A Wearing protective gloves while you are working
- B Washing your hands before eating
- C Putting barrier cream on your hands before eating
- D Washing protective gloves before each use
- E Using barrier cream for working activities

B 03

**3.07** Why should you **not** use white spirit or other solvents to clean your hands?

- A They could strip the protective oils from the skin
- B They may remove several layers of skin
- C They could block the pores of the skin
- D They could carry harmful bacteria that attack the skin

**3.08** What should you use to clean very dirty hands?

- A Soap and water
- B Thinners
- C White spirit
- D Paraffin

**3.09** How does tetanus (an infection that you can catch from contaminated land or water) get into your body?

- A Through your nose when you breathe
- B Through an open cut in your skin
- C Through your mouth when you eat or drink
- D Through the pores in your skin

**3.10** What condition can be caused by direct sunlight on bare skin?

- A Dermatitis
- B Rickets
- C Acne
- D Skin cancer

**3.11** What is the **main** issue with using barrier cream to protect your skin?

A It costs too much to use every day

B It can be broken down by some substances

C It is difficult to wash off

D It can irritate your skin and give you dermatitis

**3.12** When should you apply skin barrier cream?

A Before you start work

B When you finish work

C As part of first-aid treatment

D When you can't find your gloves

**3.13** What can cause occupational dermatitis?

A Using tools that vibrate

B Contact with another person who has dermatitis

C Contact with some strong chemicals or substances

D Working in the sun without sun cream

**3.14** Which animal is the **most** likely carrier of Weil's disease (leptospirosis) on construction sites?

A Rabbits

B Rats

C Squirrels

D Cats

**3.15** How can everyone on site help keep rats away?

A Put rat traps and poison around the site

B Ask the Local Authority to put down rat poison

C Throw food scraps over the fence or hoarding

D Put all food and drink rubbish into bins provided

**3.16** In what situation are you **most** likely to catch Weil's disease (leptospirosis)?

A If you work near wet ground, waterways or sewers

B If you work near air-conditioning units

C If you work fixing showers or baths

D If you drink water from a standpipe

**3.17** What other illness can be easily confused with the early signs of Weil's disease (leptospirosis)?

A Dermatitis

B Diabetes

C Hay fever

• D Influenza (flu)

**3.18** If your doctor has given you some medication, which of these questions is the **most** important to ask?

• A Will it make me unsafe to work or operate machinery?

B Will it make me work more slowly and earn less money?

C Will it cause me to oversleep and be late for work?

D Will I fail a drugs test if my employer asks for one?

**3.19** If you suspect someone has been drinking alcohol or is still over the alcohol limit, what should you do?

A Get them to drink plenty of strong coffee before they go back to work

• B Report the situation to your supervisor, as they may be unsafe to work

C Ask them to stay away for an hour and then go back to work

D Get them to eat and drink something, wait 30 minutes and then go back to work

**3.20** What is the **most** likely source of hepatitis in this image?

**3.21** Which of the following could be an indicator that a work colleague is feeling depressed?

A They are always smiling

• B They are quieter than usual

C They are more talkative than usual

D They are talking about work more

# 04 First aid and emergency procedures

B 04

**4.01** Where will you find out about emergency assembly points?

A A risk assessment

B A method statement

C The site induction

D The permit to work

**4.04** If the first-aid kit on site is always empty, what should you do?

A Bring your own first-aid supplies into work

B Find out who is taking all the first-aid supplies

C Inform the person who looks after the first-aid kit

D Ignore the problem as it is always the same

**4.02** How should you be informed about what to do in an emergency? Give **two** answers.

Drag your answers into the boxes below

A By attending the site induction

B By looking in the health and safety file

C By asking the Health and Safety Executive (HSE)

D By asking at the local hospital

E By reading the site noticeboards

**4.03** What should **not** be in a first-aid box?

A Bandages

B Plasters

C Safety pins

D Tablets and medicines

**4.05** Does your employer have to provide a first-aid kit?

A Yes, every site must have one

B Only if more than 50 people work on site

C Only if more than 25 people work on site

D No, there is no legal duty to provide one

**4.06** If you find an injured person and you are on your own, what is the **first** priority?

- A Inform your supervisor that someone has been injured
- B Assess the situation – do not put yourself in danger
- C Move the injured person to a safe place, and then find your supervisor
- D Ask the injured person what happened, and then find your supervisor

**4.07** If you are **not** trained in first aid, and someone is knocked unconscious, what should you do **first**?

- A Turn them over so they are lying on their back
- B Send for medical help
- C Slap their face to wake them up
- D Give them mouth-to-mouth resuscitation

**4.08** If someone has fallen from height and has no feeling in their legs, what should you do?

- A Keep their legs straight and roll them onto their back
- B Roll them onto their side and bend their legs
- C Keep them still until medical help arrives
- D Raise their legs to see if any feeling comes back

**4.09** If there is an emergency while you are on site, what should you do **first**?

- A Leave the site and go home
- B Phone home and then leave the site
- C Follow the site emergency procedure
- D Phone the Health and Safety Executive (HSE)

**4.10** If someone working in a deep inspection chamber has collapsed, what should you do **first**?

- A Get someone to lower you into the inspection chamber on a rope
- B Climb into the inspection chamber and give first-aid treatment
- C Get someone to find your supervisor while you try to rescue the worker
- D Raise the alarm and stay by the inspection chamber, but do not enter

**4.11** If someone is in contact with a live cable, what should you do **first**?

- A Phone the electricity company
- B Dial 999 and ask for an ambulance
- C Isolate the power and call for help
- D Pull them away from the cable

**4.12** If you cut your finger and it won't stop bleeding, what should you do?

A Wrap something around it and carry on working

B Tell your workmates, as you may need to rest

C Wash it, then carry on working

D Find a first aider or get other medical help

**4.13** If you think someone has broken their leg, what should you do?

A Lie them on their side in the recovery position

B Use your belt to strap their legs together

C Send for the first aider or get other help

D Lie them on their back

**4.14** If someone collapses with stomach pain and there is no first aider on site, what should you do **first**?

A Get them to sit down

B Get someone to call the emergency services

C Get them to lie down in the recovery position

D Get them to take some painkillers

**4.15** What is the one thing a first aider **cannot** do?

A Give mouth-to-mouth resuscitation

B Stop any bleeding

C Give you medicines without authorisation

D Treat you if you are unconscious

# 05 Personal protective equipment

**5.01** What should you wear if there is a risk of materials flying into your eyes?

A Tinted welding goggles

B Laser safety glasses

C Chemical-rated goggles

D Impact-rated goggles

**5.02** If you need to use a grinder or cut-off saw, what type of eye protection do you need?

A Impact-rated goggles or full face shield

B Welding goggles

C Reading glasses or sunglasses

D Light eye protection (safety glasses)

**5.03** What will safety footwear with a protective mid-sole protect you from?

A Twisting your ankle, as they have better grip than regular shoes

B Spillages, which may burn the sole of your foot

C Nails or sharp objects, which could puncture the sole of your foot if you stand on them

D Blisters, which could occur in warm, wet conditions

**5.04** When should you wear safety footwear on site?

A Only when you are working at ground level

B Until the site starts to look finished

C All the time

D Only when you are working inside

**5.05** What condition could be prevented if you wear the correct gloves while handling a hazardous substance?

A Skin disease

B Vibration white finger

C Raynaud's syndrome

D Arthritis

**5.06** Do all types of glove protect hands against chemicals?

A Yes, all gloves are made to the same standard

B Only if you put barrier cream on your hands first

C No, different gloves protect against different types of hazard

D Only if you cover the gloves with barrier cream

B
05

**5.07** If you need to wear a full body harness and you have **never** used one before, what should you do?

- A Ask for expert advice and training
- B Ask someone wearing a harness to show you what to do
- C Try to work it out for yourself
- D Read the manufacturer's instruction book

**5.08** When is the only time that you do **not** need to wear head protection on site?

- A If you are self-employed
- B If you are working alone
- C If you are in a safe area, like the site office
- D If you are working in hot weather

**5.09** How should you wear your safety helmet to get **maximum** protection from it?

- A Back to front
- B Pushed back on your head
- C Square on your head
- D Pulled forward

**5.10** What should you do if you drop your safety helmet from height onto a hard surface?

- A Repair any cracks then carry on wearing it
- B Make sure there are no cracks then carry on wearing it
- C Work without it until you can get a new one
- D Stop work until you can get a new one

**5.11** Which of the following statements about wearing a safety helmet in hot weather is **true**?

- A You can drill holes in it to keep your head cool
- B You can wear it back-to-front if it is more comfortable that way
- C You must take it off during the hottest part of the day
- D You must wear it at all times and in the right way

**5.12** When working in cold weather, what additional measures can you wear under your hard hat?

- A A baseball cap, with a peak to keep the rain out of your eyes
- B A jumper with a detachable hood
- C A woolly hat
- D Manufacturer's attachment addition for use in cold weather

**5.13** What should you do if your disposable foam earplugs keep falling out?

A. Throw them away and work without them

B. Stop work until you get more suitable ones and are shown how to fit them

C. Put two earplugs in each ear so they stay in place

D. Put rolled-up tissue paper in each ear

**5.14** What should you do if you have to raise your voice to make yourself heard on site?

A. Carry on working as it is not a problem

B. Stop work and raise it with your supervisor

C. Pack up and go home

D. Tell the person making the noise to stop work

**5.15** When **must** your employer provide you with personal protective equipment (PPE)?

A. Twice a year

B. If you pay for it

C. If it is in the contract

D. If you need to be protected

**5.16** Do you have to pay for any personal protective equipment (PPE) you need?

A. Yes, you must pay for all of it

B. Only if you need to replace lost or damaged PPE

C. Yes, but you only have to pay half the cost

D. No, your employer must pay for it

**5.17** Who should provide you with any personal protective equipment (PPE) you need, including the means to maintain it?

A. Your employer

B. You must buy your own

C. Anyone on site with a budget

D. No-one has a duty to provide it

**5.18** What should you do if your personal protective equipment (PPE) gets damaged?

A. Throw it away and work without it

B. Stop work and continue only when it has been replaced

C. Carry on wearing it but work more quickly

D. Try to repair it then carry on working

**5.19** If you have to work outdoors in bad weather, why should your employer supply you with correctly fitting waterproof clothing?

A To keep you warm and dry, so you take fewer breaks

B To protect you from the weather, as you are less likely to get muscle strains if you are warm and dry

C To keep you warm and dry, so you are less likely to catch Weil's disease (leptospirosis)

D To prevent slips, trips and falls

**5.20** Which of these statements about personal protective equipment (PPE) is **not** true?

A You must pay for any damage or loss

B You must store it correctly when you are not using it

C You must report any damage or loss to your supervisor

D You must use it as instructed

**5.21** When you start a new job, how will you know if you need any **extra** personal protective equipment (PPE)?

A By looking at your employer's health and safety policy

B You will always need it

C From the risk assessment or method statement

D By looking at the company webpage

# 06 Dust and fumes (Respiratory hazards)

**6.01** What is the biggest cause of **long-term** health issues in the construction industry?

- A Exposure to loud noise
- B Being struck by a vehicle
- C Slipping and tripping
- D Breathing in hazardous dust and fumes

**6.02** When using a power tool to cut or grind materials, why must the dust be collected and **not** allowed to get into the air?

- A To save time and avoid having to clear up the mess
- B Most dust can be harmful if breathed in
- C The tool will go faster if the dust is collected
- D A machine guard is not needed if the dust is collected

**6.04** If you have been asked to do some work that will create dust, what should you do?

- A You should not do the work because dust is highly dangerous
- B Use equipment to eliminate or reduce the dust, and wear the correct personal protective equipment (PPE)
- C Start work – no controls are needed as dust cannot cause serious harm or injury
- D Work for short periods at a time, as regular breaks will reduce the amount of dust you breathe in

**6.05** Where are you likely to breathe in the highest quantities of dust when drilling, cutting, sanding or grinding?

- A Outside on a still day
- B Outside on a windy day
- C Inside a small room
- D Inside a large space

**6.03** Work is planned that requires the use of a power tool to cut or grind materials. Select the **two** best ways to control the dust.

Drag your answers into the boxes below

- A Work slowly and carefully
- B Fit a dust extractor or collector to the machine
- C Wet cutting
- D Keep the area clean and tidy
- E Wear a dust mask

B 06

**6.06** What is the **best** way to limit exposure to dust when using a power tool?

- • A Stop dust getting into the air
- B Stand downwind of any dust
- C Do the work quickly
- D Only undertake the work during damp or wet weather

**6.07** Why is it important to be clean shaven if using a half-mask respirator?

- A Facial hair can block the filter more quickly
- B You may suffer an allergic reaction to the mask
- • C Facial hair can affect the seal around your face
- D You will be able to use the same mask for longer

**6.08** What **must** you ensure when using water to keep dust down when cutting?

- A That there is as much water as possible
- • B That the water flow is correctly adjusted
- C That somebody stands next to you to pour water from a bottle
- D That water is poured onto the surface before you start cutting

**6.09** What should you do if the water you are using to control dust runs out?

- A Put on additional respiratory protection
- • B Stop and refill the water
- C Ask everyone to clear the area and then carry on
- D Carry on but get someone to sweep up afterwards

**6.10** When drilling, cutting, sanding or grinding what is the **best** way to protect your long-term health from harmful dust?

- A Use dust extraction, or wet cut and wear a dust mask
- B Wear FFP3-rated respiratory protective equipment (RPE)
- C Wear any disposable respiratory protective equipment (RPE)
- • D Use dust extraction, or wet cut and wear FFP3-rated respiratory protective equipment (RPE)

**6.11** If you have been given a dust mask to protect you against hazardous fumes, what should you do?

- • A Do not start work until you have the correct respiratory protective equipment (RPE)
- B Do the job wearing the mask but work as quickly as you can
- C Start work without a mask but take regular breaks outside
- D Wear a second dust mask on top of the first one

**6.12** Which of the following do you **not** need to do to ensure that someone's mask works?

A Check the mask is the correct type needed

B Check the wearer has passed a face-fit test wearing the mask

C Check the mask is being worn correctly

D Check the mask under water to make sure the seals are tight

**6.13** What should you do if you need special respiratory protective equipment (RPE) to handle a chemical but no RPE has been provided?

A Get on with the job but try to work quickly

B Do not start work until you have the correct RPE and have been trained

C Start the work but take regular breaks

D Sniff the substance to see if it makes you feel ill

**6.14** Breathing in dust whilst using a cutting disc to cut through concrete could result in which of the following diseases?

A Leptospirosis

B Silicosis

C Asbestosis

D Legionnaires'

**6.15** Which of the following activities does **not** create harmful silica dust?

A Sawing timber or plywood

B Cutting kerbs, stone, paving slabs, bricks and blocks

C Breaking up concrete floors and screeds

D Chasing out walls and mortar joints or sweeping up rubble

**6.16** Which **two** materials are **most** likely to release silica dust when being cut with a rotating blade?

A Paving slabs

B Concrete blocks

C Timber

D Insulation

E Plastic pipe

**6.17** What can cause occupational asthma?

A Exposure to loud noise

B Exposure to rat urine

C Skin contact with any hazardous substance

D Breathing in hazardous dust, fumes or vapours

B 06

**6.18** What illness might you develop if you breathe in dust and fumes over long periods of time?

A Occupational lung disease

B Occupational dermatitis

C Skin cancer

D Laryngitis

**6.19** Exposure to which of the following may **not** result in lung disease?

A Asbestos

B Bird droppings

C Strong smells

D Silica dust

**6.21** What should you do if you find pigeon droppings and nests in an area where you are required to work?

A Carry on with your work carefully, so you don't disturb them

B Stop work, do not touch anything and seek advice

C Try to catch the pigeons so you can move them out of the way

D Wait for the pigeons to fly away before carrying on with your work

**6.22** Which of the following is **not** a health effect of being exposed to paints and resins which have high levels of solvents?

A Headaches and sickness

B Drowsiness or poor co-ordination

C Dermatitis or skin problems

D Muscular and skeletal disorders

**6.20** If someone is using a petrol cut-off saw (disc cutter) to cut concrete blocks near to pedestrians, what **two** immediate hazards will affect the pedestrians?

Drag your answers into the boxes below

A Flying fragments

B Contact dermatitis

C Vibration white finger

D Harmful dust

E Electric shock

# 07 Noise and vibration

**7.01** What are the symptoms and signs of noise-related hearing damage?

A There are no symptoms or signs associated with hearing damage

B Difficulty following a conversation, especially against background noise or in a crowd

C Nausea, and a skin rash around your ears

D Ear infections and regular headaches

**7.04** Can the damage by exposure to noise over a long period of time be reversed?

A Yes, with time

B Yes, if you have an operation

C No, the damage is permanent

D Yes, if you change jobs

**7.02** How can noise affect your health? Give **two** answers.

Drag your answers into the boxes below

A Temporary hearing loss

B Ear infections

C Permanent hearing loss

D Waxy ears

E Dizziness and nausea

**7.03** If you have a ringing sound in your ears after working with noisy equipment, what does this mean?

A Your hearing has been temporarily damaged

B You have also been subjected to vibration

C Your hearing protection was working properly

D The noise level was high but acceptable

**7.05** What should you do if you think noise at work may have damaged your hearing?

A Plug your ears with cotton wool to stop any more damage

B Nothing, as the damage has already been done

C Take time off work as you are unwell

D Ask your employer or doctor to arrange a hearing test

B 07

**7.06** What does wearing hearing protection do?

A Stops you hearing all noise

• B Reduces damaging noise to an acceptable level

C Repairs your hearing if it is damaged

D Helps you to hear better

**7.09** What should you do if someone near you is using noisy equipment and you have **no** hearing protection?

A Ask them to stop what they are doing as it is disrupting other workers on site

B Carry on with your work as you are not the person using the noisy equipment

• C Leave the area until you have the correct personal protective equipment (PPE)

D Speak to the other person's supervisor to stop them making the noise

**7.07** What are **two** recommended ways to protect your hearing?

Drag your answers into the boxes below

A Rolled up tissue paper in your ears

B Cotton wool pads over your ears

• C Earplugs in your ears

D Soft cloth pads over your ears

• E Ear defenders over your ears

**7.08** If you need to wear disposable foam earplugs, how should you insert them so they protect your hearing from damage?

A Soak them in water, squeeze them out and then insert them into your ear canal

B Do not roll or fold them, and insert them half way into your ear canal

• C Roll them up and insert them as far as you can, while pulling the top of your ear up to open up the ear canal

D Fold them in half, pull on your earlobe and wedge them half way into your ear

**7.10** Noise levels may be a problem, if you have to raise your voice to be understood when someone is standing how far away?

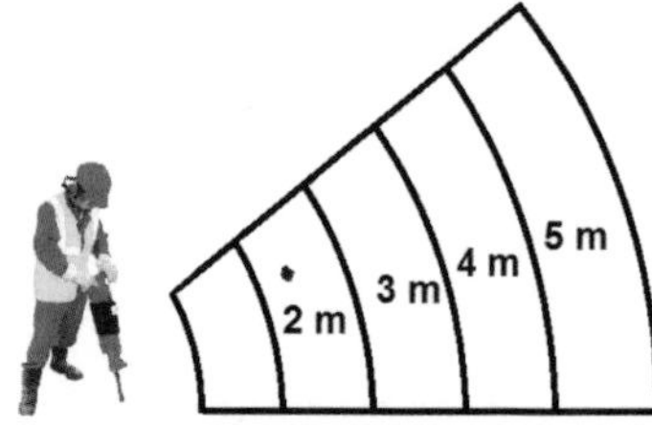

7.11 What should you do if you need to wear ear defenders but an ear pad is missing from one of the shells?

A Leave them off and work without any hearing protection

B Put them on and work with them as they are

• C Do not work in noisy areas until they are replaced

D Take an ear pad from another set of ear defenders

7.12 What **must** you do if you have to enter a hearing protection zone?

A Not make any noise

• B Wear the correct hearing protection at all times

C Take hearing protection with you in case you need to use it

D Wear hearing protection if the noise gets too loud for you

7.13 Why is over exposure to vibratory tools and equipment a serious issue?

A There are no early warning signs of damage caused by vibration

B The long-term effects of vibration are not known

C There is no way that exposure to vibration can be prevented

• D Vibration can cause disabling health conditions that cannot be cured

7.14 What is hand-arm vibration syndrome (HAVS)?

A A mild skin rash that will go away

B A serious skin condition that will not clear up

C An injury caused by severe frostbite

• D A range of conditions that can lead to permanent damage

7.15 What health problem can be caused by using hand-held vibrating tools?

A Skin cancer on your hands and arms

B An itchy skin irritation, like dermatitis

C Blisters on your hands and arms

• D Damage to the blood vessels and nerves in your fingers and hands

**7.16** What are **three** early signs of hand-arm vibration syndrome (HAVS)?

Drag your answers into the boxes below

- A Temporary loss of feeling in the fingers
- B Fingertips turn white
- C Rash on the fingers
- D Tingling or pins and needles sensation in the fingers
- E Blisters on the fingers

B
07

**7.17** You are **less** likely to suffer from hand-arm vibration syndrome (HAVS) if you feel which of the following?

- A Cold but dry
- B Cold and wet
- C Warm and dry
- D Wet but warm

**7.18** Which one of these tools is the **most** likely to cause hand-arm vibration syndrome (HAVS)?

- A Handsaw
- B Hammer drill
- C Hammer and chisel
- D Battery-powered screwdriver

**7.19** You have been using a vibrating tool and the ends of your fingers are starting to tingle. What does this mean?

- A You can carry on using the tool but you must loosen your grip
- B You must not use this tool, or any other vibrating tool, ever again
- C You need to report your symptoms before they cause a problem
- D You can carry on using the tool but you must hold it tighter

**7.20** If you have to use a vibrating tool, what would you expect your supervisor to do?

- A Measure the level of vibration every time you use the tool
- B Explain the risk assessment and the safest way and the length of time each day that you can use the tool
- C Watch you use the tool to assess the level of vibration
- D Help you to make up your own safe system of work

7.21 If you need to use a vibrating tool, even for a short time, how can you help reduce the risk of hand-arm vibration?

•A Do not grip the tool too tightly

B Hold the tool at arm's length

C Use more force

D Hold the tool more tightly

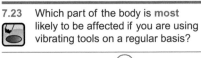

7.22 If you have to use a vibrating tool, how can you help reduce the effects of hand-arm vibration?

A Hold the tool as tightly as you can and work quickly

•B Do not smoke as it affects blood circulation

C Do the job in one long burst

D Only use one hand at a time on the tool

7.23 Which part of the body is **most** likely to be affected if you are using vibrating tools on a regular basis?

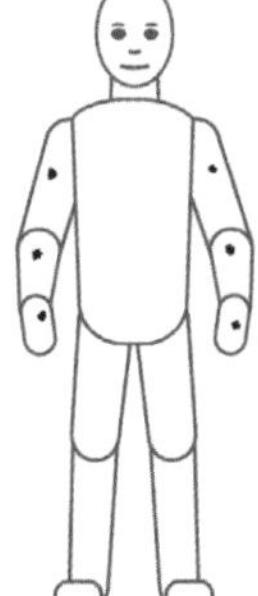

# 08 Hazardous substances

**8.01** Where are you **most** likely to come across asbestos?

- (A) In a house built between 1950 and 2005
- (B) In any building built or refurbished before the year 2000
- (C) In industrial buildings built after the year 2000
- (D) Asbestos has now been removed from all buildings

**8.02** After asbestos, which of the following causes the **most** ill health to construction workers?

- (A) Wood and MDF dust
- (B) Diesel fumes
- (C) Silica dust
- (D) Resin, solvent and paint vapours

**8.03** What illness might you develop if you breathe in asbestos dust?

- (A) Aching muscles and painful joints
- (B) Throat infections
- (C) Lung diseases
- (D) Dizziness and headaches

**8.04** Exposure to asbestos fibres may result in which illness?

- (A) Heart disease
- (B) Skin cancer
- (C) Dermatitis
- (D) Lung cancer

**8.05** How can asbestos be correctly identified?

- (A) The dust gives off a strong smell
- (B) By getting a sample analysed in a lab
- (C) By the colour of the dust
- (D) By putting a piece in water and seeing if it dissolves

**8.06** If you think you have found some asbestos, what is the **first** thing you should do?

- (A) Stop work and warn others
- (B) Take a sample to your supervisor
- (C) Put it in a bin and carry on with your work
- (D) Find the first aider

**8.07** Which **three** of the following should be labelled with this sign?

Drag your answers into the boxes below

WARNING CONTAINS ASBESTOS

Breathing asbestos dust is dangerous to health

Follow safety instructions

A Asbestos waste

B Raw asbestos

C Any product containing asbestos

D Plasterboard waste

E Recyclable waste



**8.08** Why are wet cement, mortar and concrete hazardous to your health?

A They can cause dizziness and headaches

B They can cause skin burns and dermatitis

C They can cause muscle aches

D They can cause arc eye

**8.09** Why should you wear wellington boots when working in wet cement?

A To stop your trousers getting wet

B To keep your feet warm

C To prevent dermatitis and skin burns

D To allow you to walk faster through the cement

**8.10** Which of the following provides health and safety information about a hazardous substance?

A The site diary

B The delivery note

C The COSHH assessment

D The manual handling assessment

**8.11** What does a COSHH assessment tell you?

A How to lift heavy loads and how to protect yourself

B How to work safely in confined spaces

C How a substance might harm you and how to protect yourself when you are using it

D How noise levels are assessed and how to protect your hearing

**8.12** What is the **safest** way to use a hazardous substance?

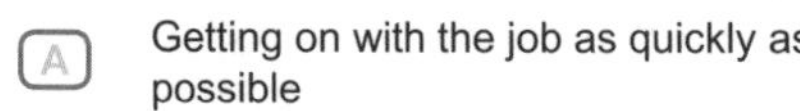

- A  Getting on with the job as quickly as possible
- B  Reading your employer's health and safety policy
- C  Understanding the COSHH assessment and following the instructions
- D  Asking someone who has already used it

**8.13** Who should explain the health risks and safe method of work you need to follow (the COSHH assessment) before you start work with a hazardous substance?

- A  A Health and Safety Executive (HSE) inspector
- B  The site first aider
- C  Your supervisor or employer
- D  The site security people

**8.15** What is the **first** thing you should do if you find an unmarked container that you think might contain chemicals?

- A  Smell it to see what it is
- B  Put it in a bin to get rid of it
- C  Move it to somewhere safe
- D  Ensure that it remains undisturbed and report it

**8.16**  What should you do if you see this label on a container or packaging?

- A  Do not use it as the substance is poisonous
- B  Find out what protection you need, as the substance is corrosive and can damage your skin upon contact
- C  Wash your hands after you have used the substance
- D  Find out what hand cleaner you will need as the substance will not wash off easily

**8.14** Where should solvents and paint be correctly stored on the site shown?

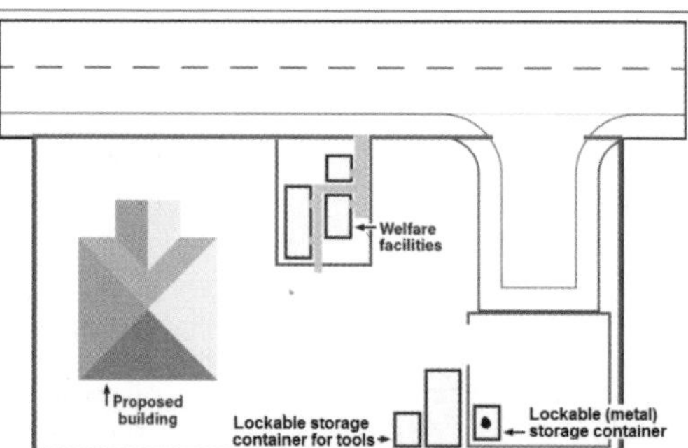

**8.17**

What should you do if you see this label on a container or packaging?

A. Find out what protection you need as the substance is harmful

B. Use it sparingly as the substance is expensive

C. Wear gloves as the substance can burn your skin

D. Do not use it as the substance is poisonous

**8.18**

How can you tell if a product is hazardous?

A. By warning symbols on the container or packaging

B. By the shape of the container

C. It will always be in a black container

D. It will always be in a cardboard box

**8.19**

What does the word **sensitiser** mean on the packaging of a substance?

A. That you could become allergic to it and have allergic reactions

B. It must be mixed with water before you can use it

C. It is perfectly safe to use without personal protective equipment (PPE)

D. It should not be used under any circumstances

**8.20**

What should you do if you see this label on a container or packaging?

A. Make sure it is stored out of the reach of children

B. Use the substance very carefully and make sure you don't spill it or splash it on yourself

C. Do not use the substance as it is poisonous

D. Find out what protection you need as the substance is toxic, even in low quantities

**8.21**

What should you do if you see this label on a container or packaging?

A. Find out how to handle the substance as it is fragile

B. Find out how to use the substance safely as it could explode

C. Find out how to use the substance safely as it is flammable (could catch fire easily)

D. Do not use the substance as it could kill you

**8.22**

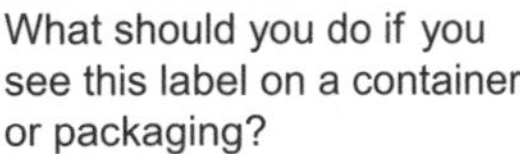

What should you do if you see this label on a container or packaging?

A. Dispose of the substance or contents by burning

B. Find out how to use the substance safely as it could explode

C. Find out how to use the substance safely as it is flammable (could catch fire easily)

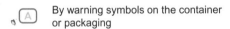

D. Warm up the contents first, with heat or a naked flame

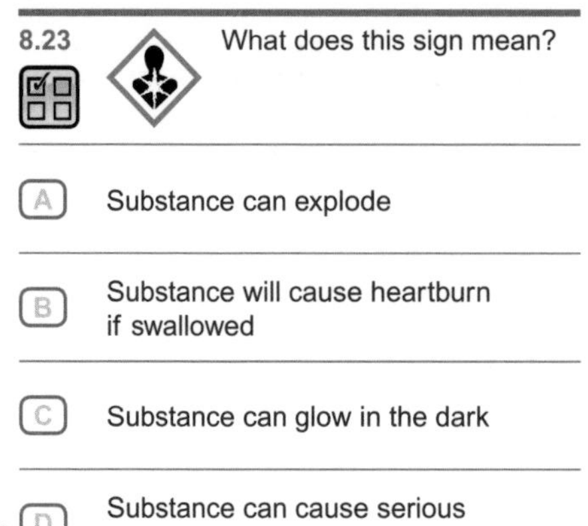

8.23 What does this sign mean?

A Substance can explode

B Substance will cause heartburn if swallowed

C Substance can glow in the dark

D Substance can cause serious long-term health hazards

B 08

# 09 Manual handling

**9.01** You are using a wheelbarrow to move a heavy load. Is this manual handling?

A No, because the wheelbarrow is carrying the load

B Only if the load slips off the wheelbarrow

C Yes, you are still manually handling the load

D Only if the wheelbarrow is pulled instead of pushed

**9.02** What is the **main** reason for ensuring safe manual handling techniques in the workplace?

A To complete the job quickly

B To prevent personal injury

C To satisfy the client's requirements

D To be prepared for safety inspections

**9.03** What is an advantage of adopting safe manual handling methods?

A You can protect your back and reduce the risk of injury

B You can increase your strength

C You can leave work earlier that day

D You can lift heavier loads

**9.04** Which part of the body is **most** likely to be injured when lifting heavy loads?

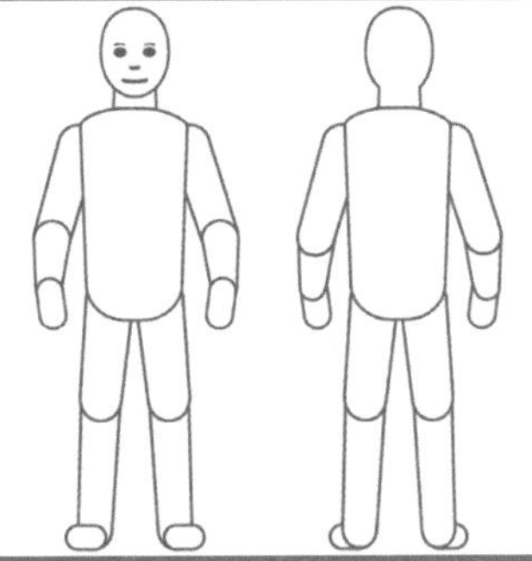

**9.05** Which part of the body is **most** likely to be injured when lifting heavy loads?

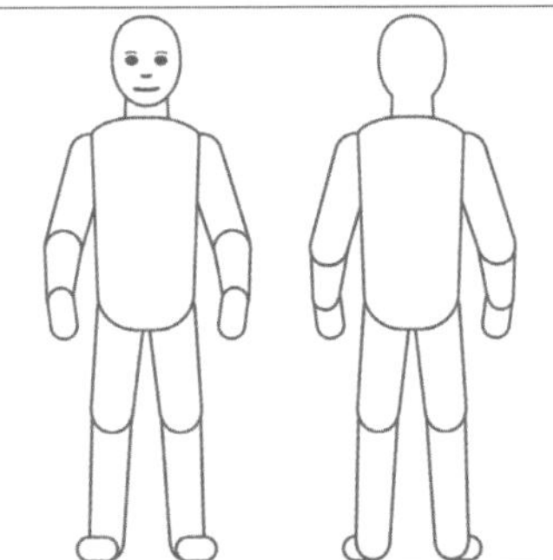

**9.06** What **must** all workers do under the regulations for manual handling?

A Wear back-support belts when lifting anything

B Make a list of all the heavy things they have to carry

C Lift any size of load once the risk assessment has been done

D Follow their employer's safe systems of work

B 09

**9.07** Who should be involved in planning the safe system of work for your manual handling?

A You and your colleagues

B Your supervisor or employer

C You and your supervisor or employer

D The Health and Safety Executive (HSE)

**9.10** If you have to lift a heavy load, what **must** your employer do?

A Make sure your supervisor is there to advise while you lift

B Do a risk assessment of the task

C Nothing, it is part of your job to lift loads

D Watch you while you lift the load

**9.08** What **three** of the following factors must you think about to lift a load safely?

Drag your answers into the boxes below

A Its size and shape

B Its weight

C How to grip or hold it firmly

D Whether the content is insured

E What the value of it is

**9.09** What **two** things are important for the use of manual handling lifting aids?

Drag your answers into the boxes below

A The user must hold a CSCS card

B The lifting aid can only be used outside

C The lifting aid must be designed for the task

D The lifting aid must not be more than six months old

E The user must be trained in the correct use of the lifting aid

**9.11** You need to move a load that might be too heavy for you. What **three** methods could you use?

Drag your answers into the boxes below

- A Dividing the load into smaller loads if possible
- B Getting someone to help you
- C Using an aid, such as a trolley or wheelbarrow
- D Testing the load's weight by picking it up for a short time
- E Dragging the load to avoid lifting it



**9.12** You have to move a load that might be too heavy for you. You cannot divide it into smaller parts and there is no-one to help you. What should you do?

- A Do not move the load until you have a safe way of doing it
- B Get a forklift truck, even though you have not been trained to use it
- C Try to lift it using the correct lifting methods
- D Lift and move the load quickly to avoid injury

**9.13** What are **two** risks of carrying a load in cold, damp conditions?

- A Your ability to carry the load safely will be reduced
- B The path could be slippery
- C You will need to work more quickly to warm up
- D The load will be easier to carry
- E The load will feel lighter due to the cold conditions

**9.14** You are using a trolley to move a heavy load a long distance but a wheel comes off. What should you do?

- A Carry the load the rest of the way
- B Ask someone to help you pull the trolley the rest of the way
- C Drag the trolley on your own the rest of the way
- D Find another way to move the load

**9.15** You need to lift a load that is not heavy, but it is so big that you cannot see in front of you. What should you do?

- A Ask someone to help carry the load so that you can both see ahead
- B Get someone to walk next to you and give directions
- C Get someone to walk in front of you and tell others to get out of the way
- D Move the load on your own because it is so large that anyone in your way is sure to see it

**9.16** What should you do if you have to carry a load down a steep slope?

A Walk backwards down the slope to help you balance

B Carry the load on your shoulder

C Assess whether you can still carry the load safely

D Put the load down and let gravity move it down the slope

**9.17** What should you do if you have been told how to lift a heavy load, but you think there is a better way to do it?

A Ignore what you have been told and do it your way

B Ask your workmates to decide which way you should do it

C Discuss your idea with your supervisor

D Forget your idea and do it the way you have been told

**9.18** Your new job involves some manual handling but an old injury means that you have a weak back. What should you do?

A Tell your supervisor you can lift anything

B Tell your supervisor that lifting might be a problem

C Try some lifting then tell your supervisor about your back

D Tell your supervisor about your back if it gets injured again

**9.19** What is the outcome of wearing a back support belt when lifting?

A You can lift any load without being injured

B You can safely lift more than usual

C You could face the same risk of injury as when you are not wearing one

D You will crush your backbone and damage it

**9.20** What does it mean if you have to twist or turn your body when you lift and place a load?

A The weight you can lift safely will be less than usual

B The weight you can lift safely will be more than usual

C You can lift the same weight as usual

D You must wear a back brace

**9.21** If you need to reach above your head to place a load or lower a load to the floor, which of these is **not** true?

A It will be more difficult to keep your back straight and chin tucked in

B You will put extra stress on your arms and your back

C You can safely handle more weight than usual

D The load will be more difficult to control

**9.22** If you have to move a load while you are sitting down, how much can you lift safely?

A Less than the usual amount

B The usual amount

C Twice the usual amount

D Three times the usual amount

**9.23** If you need to move a load that is heavier on one side than the other, how should you pick it up?

A With the heavy side towards you

B With the heavy side away from you

C With the heavy side on your strong arm

D With the heavy side on your weak arm

**9.24** Which of the following is the **best** method to help minimise the risk of injury when manual handling?

A Safely using lifting aids

B Making the area of site flatter before performing the task

C Asking a trained person to carry the load

D Not having any heavy objects on site

**9.25** What is the **main** reason for using lifting aids when undertaking a manual handling activity?

A They help reduce the risk of personal injury

B You do not require training to use them

C You can lift any load when using them

D They are expensive and should be used

# C
# General safety

## Contents

# 10 Safety signs

**10.01** What are blue and white signs?

- (A) Mandatory signs – meaning you must do something
- (B) Prohibition signs – meaning you must not do something
- (C) Warning signs – alerting you to hazards or danger
- (D) Safe condition signs – giving you information

**10.02** What does this sign mean?

- (A) Wear hearing protection if you want to
- (B) You must wear hearing protection
- (C) No personal electronic devices
- (D) Caution – noisy machinery

**10.03** What does this sign mean?

- (A) Safety glasses cleaning station
- (B) Warning – bright lights or lasers
- (C) Caution – poor lighting
- (D) You must wear eye protection

**10.04** What does this sign mean?

- (A) Safety boots or safety shoes must be worn
- (B) Wellington boots must be worn
- (C) Be aware of slip and trip hazards
- (D) No dirty footwear past this point

**10.05** What does this sign mean?

- (A) You must carry safety gloves at all times
- (B) Dispose of used safety gloves here
- (C) Safety gloves do not need to be worn
- (D) Safety gloves must be worn

**10.06** What does this sign mean?

- (A) Only white safety helmets allowed in this area
- (B) Remove safety helmets in this area
- (C) Safety helmets must be worn
- (D) Dispose of damaged safety helmets here

**10.07** Which sign is categorised as a mandatory sign?

A

B

C

D

**10.08**  What are round red and white signs with a diagonal line?

A Mandatory signs – meaning you must do something

B Prohibition signs – meaning you must not do something

C Warning signs – alerting you to hazards or danger

D Safe condition signs – giving you information

**10.09**  What does this sign mean?

A Smoking is allowed

B Danger – flammable materials present

C No smoking

D No explosives or naked flames

**10.10**  What does this sign mean?

A No lone working

B No entry without a hard hat

C No access for pedestrians

D No entry during the day

**10.11**  What does this sign mean?

A Do not use the tap

B Not for washing

C Not drinkable

D Do not wash your vehicle

**10.12**  What does this sign mean?

A No gloves

B Do not touch

C Stop button

D Use the handrail

**10.13**  What does this sign mean?

A No mobile phones

B Wifi enabled area

C Mobile phones are allowed

D Mobile phone charging point

**10.14** Which sign is categorised as a prohibition sign?

A

B

C

D

**10.15**  What are green and white signs?

A Mandatory signs – meaning you must do something

B Prohibition signs – meaning you must not do something

C Warning signs – alerting you to hazards or danger

D Safe condition signs – giving you information

**10.16**  What does this sign mean?

A It tells you where the canteen is located

B It tells you which direction to walk

C It tells you where to assemble in case of an emergency

D It tells you where the site induction room is located

**10.17** 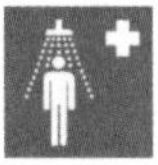 What does this sign mean?

A Toilets and shower facilities

B Drying area for wet weather clothes

C Emergency shower

D Fire sprinklers above

**10.18**  What does this sign mean?

A Escape route or emergency exit is to the right

B Open the door by sliding it to the right

C One-way pedestrian route

D The site entrance is to the right

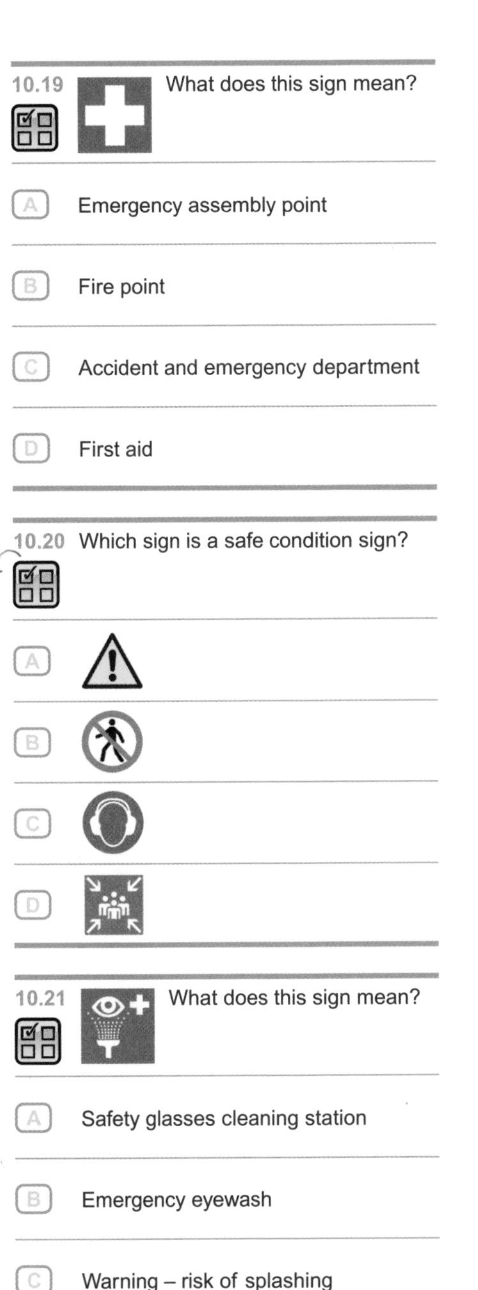

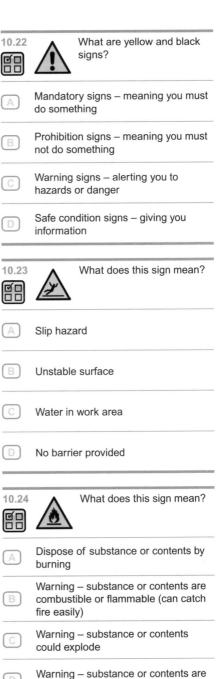

**10.19** What does this sign mean?

(A) Emergency assembly point

(B) Fire point

(C) Accident and emergency department

(D) First aid

**10.20** Which sign is a safe condition sign?

(A)

(B)

(C)

(D)

**10.21** What does this sign mean?

(A) Safety glasses cleaning station

(B) Emergency eyewash

(C) Warning – risk of splashing

(D) Wear eye protection

**10.22** What are yellow and black signs?

(A) Mandatory signs – meaning you must do something

(B) Prohibition signs – meaning you must not do something

(C) Warning signs – alerting you to hazards or danger

(D) Safe condition signs – giving you information

**10.23** What does this sign mean?

(A) Slip hazard

(B) Unstable surface

(C) Water in work area

(D) No barrier provided

**10.24** What does this sign mean?

(A) Dispose of substance or contents by burning

(B) Warning – substance or contents are combustible or flammable (can catch fire easily)

(C) Warning – substance or contents could explode

(D) Warning – substance or contents are harmful

**10.25** What does this sign mean?

A Radioactive material

B Warning – rotating object

C High voltage

D Warning – laser beams

**10.26** What does this sign mean?

A Plant operators wanted

B Industrial vehicles operating

C Manual handling is not allowed

D Storage area

**10.28** Which sign is warning you about a slippery surface?

A 

B  

C 

D 

**10.29** Which sign is a warning about high voltage electricity?

A   

B  

C  

D  

**10.27** Where should this sign be displayed?

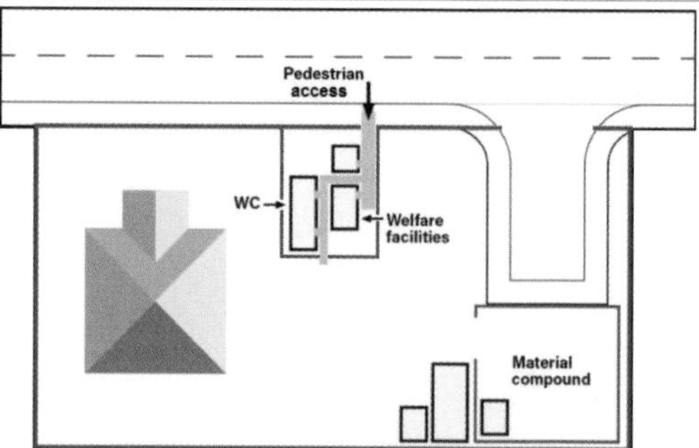

**10.30** Which sign is categorised as a warning sign?

A 
B 
C 
D

**10.31**  What does this sign mean?

A Assemble here in the event of a fire
B Fire extinguishers and fire-fighting equipment kept here
C Parking reserved for emergency service vehicles
D Do not store flammable materials here

**10.32**  What does this sign mean?

A Fire alarm call point
B Hot surface – do not touch
C Wear flameproof hand protection
D Emergency light switch

**10.33**  What does this sign mean?

A Press here to sound the fire alarm
B Fire hose reel located here
C Turn key to open fire door
D Do not use if there is a fire

**10.34** Which sign means that a substance is toxic if swallowed or inhaled?

A 
B 
C 
D

**10.35** Which sign means that a substance could cause damage to your organs if inhaled?

A 
B 
C 
D

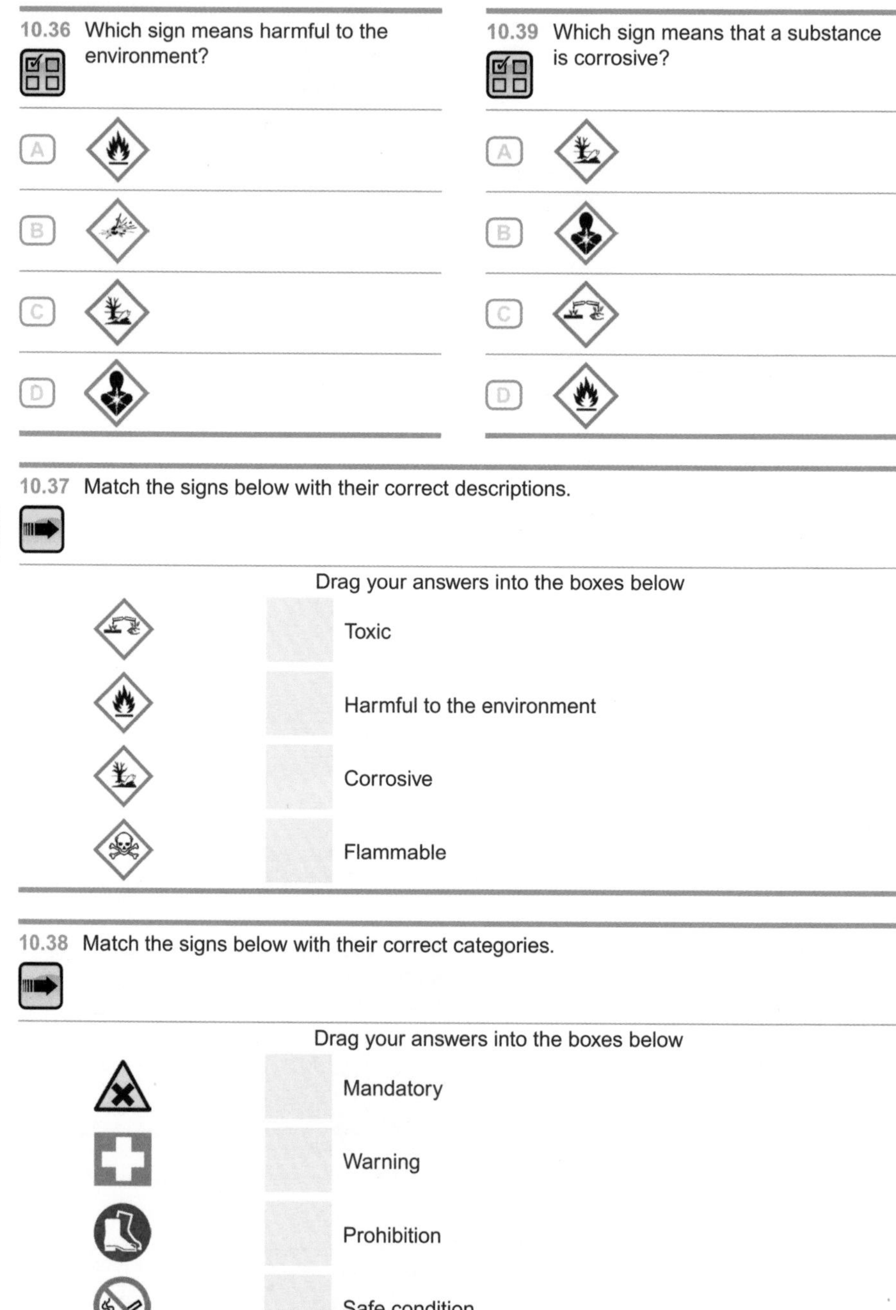

10.36 Which sign means harmful to the environment?

A

B

C

D

10.39 Which sign means that a substance is corrosive?

A

B

C

D

10.37 Match the signs below with their correct descriptions.

Drag your answers into the boxes below

Toxic

Harmful to the environment

Corrosive

Flammable

10.38 Match the signs below with their correct categories.

Drag your answers into the boxes below

Mandatory

Warning

Prohibition

Safe condition

**10.40** Match the signs below with their correct categories.

Drag your answers into the boxes below

 Prohibition

 Mandatory

 Safe condition

 Warning

**10.41** Match the signs below with their correct categories.

Drag your answers into the boxes below

 Prohibition

 Mandatory

 Safe condition

 Warning

**10.42** Match the signs below with their correct categories.

Drag your answers into the boxes below

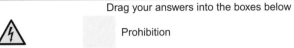

 Prohibition

 Mandatory

 Safe condition

 Warning

10.43 Match the signs below with their correct categories.

Drag your answers into the boxes below

Prohibition

Mandatory

Safe condition

Warning



10.44 Match the signs below with their correct categories.

Drag your answers into the boxes below

Prohibition

Mandatory

Safe condition

Warning

10.45 Match the signs below with their correct categories.

Drag your answers into the boxes below

Prohibition

Mandatory

Safe condition

Warning

10.46 Match the signs below with their correct categories.

Drag your answers into the boxes below

| Sign | | Category |
|---|---|---|
| | | Prohibition |
| | | Mandatory |
| | | Safe condition |
| | | Warning |

# 11 Fire prevention and control

**11.01** What are **two** common fire risks on construction sites?

Drag your answers into the boxes below

A. 230 volt power tools

B. Poor housekeeping and build up of waste

C. Timber racks

D. Uncontrolled hot works

E. 110 volt extension reels

C
11

**11.02** What is the fire assembly point?

A. Where fire engines must go when they arrive on site

B. Where the fire extinguishers are kept

C. Where people must go when the fire alarm sounds

D. Where the fire started

**11.03** In addition to heat, what other **two** factors must be present to enable a fire to start?

Drag your answers into the boxes below

A. Nitrogen

B. Argon

C. Oxygen

D. Carbon dioxide

E. Fuel

HEAT

**11.04** How would you expect to find out the location of the fire assembly point?

A During a visit by the Health and Safety Executive (HSE)

B During site induction

C By reading your employer's health and safety policy

D Your colleagues will tell you

**11.05** If you discover a fire, what is the **first** thing you should do?

A Put your tools away

B Finish what you are doing, if it is safe to do so

C Try to put out the fire

D Raise the alarm

**11.06** Where should you go if you hear the fire alarm?

A To the site canteen

B To the assembly point

C To the site office

D To the site welfare facilities

**11.07** A large fire has been reported. You have **not** been trained to use fire extinguishers. What should you do?

A Put away all your tools and then go to the assembly point

B Report to the site office and then go home

C Go straight to the assembly point

D Leave work for the day

**11.08** What **must** you check if you need to work in a corridor that is a fire escape route?

A That your tools and equipment do not block the route

B That all doors into the corridor are locked

C That you only use spark-proof tools

D That you remove all fire escape signs before you start

**11.09** What does it mean if you see frost around the valve on a liquefied petroleum gas (LPG) cylinder?

A The cylinder is nearly empty

B The cylinder is full

C The valve is leaking

D You must lay the cylinder on its side

**11.10** Which **two** extinguishers should **not** be used on electrical fires?

A Dry powder (blue colour band)

B Foam (cream colour band)

C Water (red colour band)

D Carbon dioxide (black colour band)

**11.13** What does a hot-work permit allow you to do?

A Work in hot weather

B Carry out work that needs warm, protective clothing

C Carry out work that could start a fire

D Light a bonfire



**11.11** If your job needs a hot-work permit, what **two** things would you expect to have to do?

Drag your answers into the boxes below

A Have a fire extinguisher close to the work

B Check for signs of fire when you stop work

C Know where all the fire extinguishers are kept on site

D Write a site evacuation plan

E Know how to refill fire extinguishers

**11.12** Which **two** of these activities are likely to need a hot-work permit?

Drag your answers into the boxes below

A Cutting steel with an angle grinder

B Using the heaters in the drying room

C Refuelling a diesel dump truck

D Replacing an empty liquefied petroleum gas (LPG) cylinder with a full one

E Soldering pipework in a central heating system

# 12 Electrical safety, tools and equipment

12.01 What two things should you do to reduce trips and injuries caused by untidy leads and extension cables?

Drag your answers into the boxes below

A Run cables and leads above head height and over the top of doorways and walkways

B Tie any excess cables and leads up into the smallest coil possible

C Keep trailing cables and leads close to the wall

D Make sure your cables have not been used before

E Only use thinner 230 volt extension cables

12.02 What two things must you do if you need to use an extension cable?

Drag your answers into the boxes below

A Only uncoil the length of cable you need

B Uncoil the whole cable

C Clean the cable with a damp cloth

D Check the whole cable and connectors for damage

E Only check the part of the cable you need for damage

12.03 What is the best way to protect an extension cable and also reduce trip hazards?

A Run the cable above head height

B Run the cable by the shortest route

C Cover the cable with yellow tape

D Cover the cable with pieces of wood

12.04 What should you do if an extension cable has a cut in its outer cover?

A Check the copper wires aren't showing in the cut and then use the cable

B Put electrical tape around the damaged part

C Report the fault and make sure no-one else uses the cable

D Put a bigger fuse in the cable plug

**12.05** What **two** things should you do if you need to run an electrical cable across an area used by vehicles?

Drag your answers into the boxes below

A Wrap the cable in yellow tape so that drivers can see it

B Cover the cable with a protective ramp

C Cover the cable with scaffold boards

D Put up a sign that says 'Ramp ahead'

E Run the cable at head height



**12.06** Do you need to inspect simple hand tools like trowels, screwdrivers, saws and hammers?

A No, never

B Yes, if they have not been used for a couple of weeks

C Yes, they should be checked each time you use them

D Only if someone else has borrowed them

**12.07** You need to work near an electric cable. The cable has bare wires. What should you do?

A Quickly touch the cable to see if it is live

B Check there are no sparks coming from the cable and then start work

C Tell your supervisor and keep well away

D Push the cable out of the way so that you can start work

**12.08** What is the **main** danger of using a chisel or bolster with a mushroomed head?

A It will shatter and send fragments flying into the air

B You are more likely to hit your hand with the chisel head

C The shaft of the chisel will bend, putting a strain on your wrist

D The hammer could slip off the head of the bolster or chisel

**12.09** What should you do if the head on your hammer comes loose?

A Stop work and get the hammer repaired or replaced

B Find another heavy tool to use instead of the hammer

C Keep using it but be aware that the head could come off at any time

D Tell the other people near you to keep out of the way

**12.10** You are in a gang using an insulated pick to break up the surface. What **two** things should you be aware of?

Drag your answers into the boxes below

A. Standing too close to the worker with the pick

B. Smoking, as gas could be released

C. Whether the ganger is watching you

D. Standing with your hands in your pockets

E. Standing in front of or behind the worker with the pick

**12.11** What requirement **must** you meet to operate a power tool?

A. You must be over 18 years old

B. You must have a gold CSCS card

C. You must be trained and competent

D. You must only operate it when your supervisor is present

**12.13** Why **must** you be fully trained before you use a cartridge-operated tool?

A. They are heavy and could cause manual handling injuries

B. They operate like a gun and can be dangerous in inexperienced hands

C. They can cause dermatitis when used

D. They have exposed electrical parts

**12.12** What are the **two** main functions of the guards on cutting and grinding machines?

Drag your answers into the boxes below

A. To stop materials getting onto the blade or wheel

B. To give you a firm handhold

C. To balance the machine

D. To stop fragments flying into the air

E. To stop you coming into contact with the blade or wheel

**12.14** What should you do if the guard is missing from a power tool?

A Try to make another guard

B Use the tool but try to work quickly

C Not use the tool until a proper guard has been fitted

D Use the tool but work carefully and slowly

**12.15** What should you do if you need to use a power tool with a rotating blade?

A Remove the guard so that you can clearly see the blade

B Adjust the guard to expose just enough blade to let you do the job

C Remove the guard but wear leather gloves to protect your hands

D Adjust the guard to expose the maximum amount of blade

**12.16** What should you do before you adjust an electric hand tool?

A Switch it off but leave the plug in the socket

B Switch it off and remove the plug from the socket

C You should never adjust an electric hand tool yourself

D Put tape over the power switch

**12.17** Which **two** of the following statements about power tools are **true**?

A Always carry the tool by its cord

B Always unplug the tool by pulling its cord

C Always unplug the tool when you are not using it

D Always leave the tool plugged in when you check or adjust it

E You must be trained and competent before using any power tool

**12.18** What should you do if the electrical equipment you are using cuts out?

A Shake it to see if it will start again

B Pull the electric cable to see if it is loose

C Switch the power off and on a few times

D Switch off the power and look for signs of damage

12.19 You need to use an air-powered tool. What **three** hazards are likely to affect you?

Drag your answers into the boxes below

A Electric shock

B Hand-arm vibration

C Airborne dust and flying fragments

D Leaking air hoses

E Radiation

12.20 If someone near you is using a petrol cut-off saw (disc cutter) to cut concrete blocks, what **three** immediate hazards are likely to affect you?

Drag your answers into the boxes below

A Flying fragments

B Contact dermatitis

C Harmful dust in the air

D High noise levels

E Vibration white finger

12.21 You have been asked to dig to expose power cables. You have been given a cable avoiding tool (CAT) to detect them but you haven't been shown how to use it. What should you do?

A Dig the hole without it

B Ask a colleague to show you how to use it

C Read the manual before you start work

D Tell your supervisor you haven't been trained

12.22 Why is it dangerous to run an abrasive wheel faster than its recommended **maximum** speed?

A The wheel will get clogged and stop

B The motor could burst into flames

C The wheel could shatter into many pieces

D The safety guard cannot be used

**12.23** What **two** main visual inspections should you carry out before using a power tool?

Drag your answers into the boxes below

A. Check the carry case isn't broken

B. Check the power lead, plug and casing are in good condition

C. Check the manufacturer's label hasn't come off

D. Check switches and triggers, and make sure guards are adjusted and work correctly

E. Check it is marked with a security stamp



**12.24** You have been asked to use a hand tool or power tool on site. You know that it is the right tool for the job. What else **must** you check?

A. That it was made in the UK

B. That it is inspected at the start of each week

C. That it was bought from a builders' merchant

D. That it is inspected before you use it

**12.25** When do you need to check tools and equipment for damage?

A. Each time before use

B. Every day

C. Once a week

D. At least once a year

**12.26** You are using a power tool with a portable appliance testing (PAT) label on it. What information should be on the label?

A. When the tool was passed as safe, and when it was tested

B. When the tool was made

C. Who tested the tool when it left the factory

D. The tool's earth-loop impedance

**12.27** Why should you **never** store batteries loose in your tool bag?

A. You might forget to charge them

B. Your tool bag will be heavy and damage your back

C. If the terminals short out, they could cause a fire

D. They give off a poisonous gas in a confined space

**12.28** Why should you try to use battery-powered tools rather than electrical ones?

A They are cheaper to run

B They will not give you a serious electric shock

C They will not give you hand-arm vibration

D They do not need to be tested or serviced

**12.29** What is the recommended safe voltage for electrical equipment on building sites?

A 12 volts

B 24 volts

C 110 volts

D 230 volts

**12.30** Why do building sites use a 110 volt electricity supply instead of a 230 volt domestic supply?

A It is cheaper

B It is less likely to kill you

C It moves faster along the cables

D It is safer for the environment

**12.31** What colour is a 110 volt power cable and connector?

A Black

B Red

C Blue

D Yellow

**12.32** Why should you use a residual current device (RCD) with 230 volt tools?

A It lowers the voltage

B It quickly cuts off the power if there is a fault

C It makes the tool run at a safe speed

D It saves energy and lowers costs

**12.33** How do you check if a residual current device (RCD) connected to a power tool is working?

A Switch the tool on and off

B Press the test button on the RCD

C Use a hand-held RCD test meter

D Run the tool at top speed to see if it cuts out

**12.34** You need to use a 230 volt item of equipment. How should you protect yourself from an electric shock?

A) Use a generator

B) Put up safety screens around you

C) Use a portable residual current device (RCD)

D) Wear rubber boots and gloves

**12.35** Which item of equipment would **not** require portable appliance testing (PAT)?

A) 110 volt transformer

B) Battery-powered rechargeable drill

C) 110 volt extension lead

D) Plug in portable halogen light

**12.36** Which item of equipment would **not** require portable appliance testing (PAT)?

A) 110 volt transformer

B) Hammer and bolster

C) 110 volt extension lead

D) Plug in breaker

**12.37** When is it safe to work close to an overhead power line?

A) If you do not touch the line for more than 30 seconds

B) If you use a wooden ladder

C) If the power is switched off

D) If it is not raining

**12.38** You are using a generator to power some lighting when a lamp blows. You have a spare lamp. What should you do?

A) Disconnect the lighting from the generator before replacing the lamp

B) Wait for a fully qualified electrician with a NICEIC card

C) Replace the lamp without disconnecting the generator, as you can't get a shock from it

D) Carry on working in the dark

# 13 Site transport safety and lifting operations

13.01 What are the **two** conditions for being able to operate plant on site?

Drag your answers into the boxes below

A You must be trained and competent

B You must be authorised

C You must be over 21 years old

D You must hold a full driving licence

E You must hold a British passport

13.02 Your supervisor asks you to drive a dumper truck. You have **never** driven one before. What should you do?

A Ask a trained driver how to operate it

B Tell your supervisor that you are not trained so cannot operate it

C Watch other dumpers to see how they are operated

D Operate the dumper in an open area in case you make a mistake

13.03 How would you expect to be told about the site traffic rules?

A During the site induction

B By a Health and Safety Executive (HSE) inspector

C By a note on a noticeboard

D By other workers on site

13.04 How would you expect a well-organised site to keep pedestrians away from traffic routes?

A The site manager will direct all pedestrians away from traffic routes

B The traffic routes will be shown on the health and safety law poster

C There will be barriers between traffic and pedestrian routes

D There is no need to keep traffic and pedestrians apart

13.05 When is a site vehicle **most** likely to injure pedestrians?

A While reversing

B While lifting materials onto scaffolds

C While tipping into an excavation

D While digging out footings

**13.06** Why should you **never** walk behind a lorry when it is reversing?

A Most lorries are not fitted with mirrors

B The driver is unlikely to know you are there

C Most lorry drivers aren't very good at reversing

D You will need to run, not walk, to get past it in time

**13.07** The quickest way to your work area is through a contractor's vehicle compound. Which way should you go?

A Around the compound if vehicles are moving

B Straight through the compound if no vehicles appear to be moving

C Around the compound every time

D Straight through the compound if no-one is looking

**13.08** When is site transport allowed to drive along a pedestrian route?

A During meal breaks

B If it is the shortest route

C Only if necessary and if all pedestrians are excluded

D Only if the vehicle has a flashing yellow light

**13.09** Which of the following is bad practice when organising site transport?

A Speed limits

B Barriers to keep pedestrians away from mobile plant and vehicles

C Pedestrians and mobile plant using the same routes

D One-way systems

**13.10** A forklift truck is blocking the way to where you want to go on site. It is lifting materials onto a scaffold. What should you do?

A Only walk under the raised load if you are wearing a safety helmet

B Catch the driver's attention and then walk under the raised load

C Start to run so that you are not under the load for very long

D Wait or go around, but never walk under a raised load

**13.11** When you walk across the site, what is the **best** way to avoid an accident with mobile plant?

A Keep to the designated pedestrian routes

B Ride on the plant

C Get the attention of the driver before you get too close

D Wear hi-vis clothing

**13.12** You need to walk past a 360° mobile crane. The crane is operating near a wall. What is the **main** danger?

A The crane could crash into the wall

B You could be crushed if you walk between the crane and the wall

C You could get whole-body vibration from the crane

D Your hearing could be damaged by high noise levels from the crane

**13.13** You are walking across the site. A large mobile crane reverses across your path. What should you do?

A Help the driver to reverse

B Start to run so that you can pass behind the reversing crane

C Pass close to the front of the crane

D Wait or find another way around the crane

**13.14** What should you do if you need to walk past someone using a mobile crane?

A Guess what the crane operator will do next and squeeze by

B Try to catch the attention of the crane operator

C Run to get past the crane quickly

D Take another route so that you stay clear of the crane

**13.15** When can a mobile plant operator let people ride in, or on, the machine?

A Only if they have a long way to walk

B As long as the site speed limit is not exceeded

C Only if it is designed to carry passengers and has a designated seat

D Only if the cab door is shut

**13.16** You think some mobile plant is operating too close to where you have to work. What should you do **first**?

A Stop work and speak to the plant operator

B Stop work and speak to the plant operator's supervisor

C Look out for the plant and carry on working

D Stop work and speak to your own supervisor

**13.17** What should you do if you see a dumper being driven too fast?

A Keep out of its way and report it

B Try to catch the dumper and speak to the driver

C Report it to the police

D Do nothing as dumpers are allowed to go above the site speed limit

**13.18** You see a lorry parking. It has a flat tyre. Why should you tell the driver?

A The lorry will use more fuel

B The lorry will need to travel at a much slower speed

C The lorry could be unsafe to drive

D The lorry can only carry small loads

**13.19** An excavator has just stopped work. Liquid is dripping and forming a small pool under the back of the machine. What could this mean?

A It is normal for fluids to vent after the machine stops

B The machine is hot so the diesel has expanded and overflowed

C Someone put too much diesel into the machine before it started work

D The machine has a leak and could be unsafe

**13.20** You see a driver refuelling an excavator but most of the diesel is spilling onto the ground. What is the **first** thing you should do?

A Tell your supervisor the next time you see them

B Tell the driver immediately and locate the spill kit

C Look around for a spill kit and then tell your supervisor

D Do nothing, as the diesel will eventually seep into the ground

**13.21** You think a load is about to fall from a moving forklift truck. What should you do?

A Keep clear but try to warn the driver and others in the area

B Run alongside the machine and try to hold on to the load

C Run and tell your supervisor

D Sound the nearest fire alarm bell

**13.22** A truck has to tip materials into a trench. Who should give signals to the truck driver?

A Anyone who is wearing a hi-vis coat

B Someone standing in the trench

C Someone who knows the signals

D Only the person who is trained and appointed for the job

**13.23** You see a mobile crane lifting a load. The load is about to hit something. What should you do?

A Go and tell your supervisor

B Try and warn the person supervising or banking the lift

C Go and tell the crane driver

D Do nothing and assume everything is under control

13.24 A crane has to do a difficult lift. The signaller asks you to help, but you are **not** trained in plant signals. What should you do?

A Politely refuse and explain you don't know how to signal

B Start giving signals to the crane driver

C Only help if the signaller really can't manage alone

D Ask the signaller to show you what signals to use

13.25 What do you need before you can supervise any lift using a crane?

A A mobile phone so you can talk to the crane driver

B You must be trained and assessed as competent

C Written instructions from the crane hire company

D Nothing – the crane driver will tell you what to do

C
13

# D
# High risk activities

**Contents**

# 14 Working at height

**14.01** Which type of accident kills the **most** construction workers?

A Falling from height

B Contact with electricity

C Being run over by site transport

D Being hit by a falling object

**14.04** How is working at height usually defined?

A Working 1.2 m above the ground or higher

B Working 2 m above the ground or higher

C Working at any height that would cause an injury if you fell

D Working 3 m above the ground or higher

**14.02** What are **two** of your responsibilities when working at height?

Drag your answers into the boxes below

A Ensure you are sufficiently trained

B Make use of access equipment

C Throw things to your colleague below

D Ignore the safety briefing given by your supervisor

E Climb up the outside of the scaffolding

**14.03** What should you do if you feel that a task working at height is unsafe?

A Carry on working and tell your supervisor when you next see them

B Work the problem out for yourself

C Stop working immediately and report it to your supervisor

D Borrow some work equipment from another job

**14.05** What should you do if you are required to use access equipment that you have **not** been trained to use?

A Do the job if it won't take long

B Get a ladder instead

C Stop work and speak to your supervisor

D Ask someone else to do it

D 14

**14.06** What is the **main** regulation that controls the use of suitable access equipment for working at height?

A HSG33 Health and Safety in Roofwork

B Lifting Operations and Lifting Equipment Regulations

C Work at Height Regulations

D Workplace (Health, Safety and Welfare) Regulations

**14.07** According to the Work at Height Regulations when **can** you use a ladder at work?

A If it is long enough

B You must never use a ladder on site

C If other people do not need to use it for access

D If you are doing low risk work for a short time

**14.08** What angle should a leaning ladder be used at?

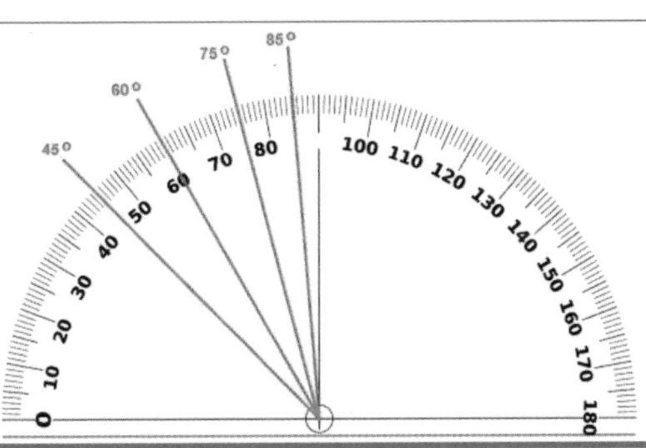


**14.09** Who should check a ladder before it is used?

A The person who is going to use it

B A supervisor

C The site safety officer

D The manufacturer

**14.10** What is the **best** way to make sure that a ladder is secure and won't slip?

A Tie it at the top

B Ask someone to stand with their foot on the bottom rung

C Tie it at the bottom

D Wedge the bottom of the ladder with blocks of wood

**14.11** What should you do when you are climbing a ladder?

A Have three points of contact with the ladder at all times

B Have two points of contact with the ladder at all times

C Only use the ladder whilst wearing a safety harness

D Have two people on the ladder at all times

**14.12** A scaffold guard-rail **must** be removed to allow you to carry out a task. If you are not a scaffolder, can you remove the guard-rail?

A Yes, if you put it back as soon as you have finished

B Yes, if you put it back before you leave site

C No, only a scaffolder can remove the guard-rail but you can put it back

D No, only a scaffolder can remove the guard-rail and put it back

**14.13** How many people should be on a ladder at the same time?

A Only one person

B A maximum of two people

C One person on each section of an extension ladder

D Three people, if it is long enough

**14.14** What should you do if you find a ladder that is damaged?

A Don't use it and make sure that others know about the damage

B Don't use it and report the damage at the end of your shift

C Try to mend the damage before using it

D Use it if you can avoid the damaged part

**14.15** Which of the following is **not** true when using podium steps?

A Podium step wheels must be locked before you get on

B Podium steps can easily topple if you over reach sideways

C Podium steps are safe and can't topple over

D Podium steps are work equipment and must be inspected before use and every seven days

**14.16** Which image shows the **safest** method when using a stepladder?

**14.17** Which image shows the safe use of a ladder?

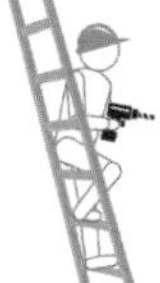

**14.18** You need to use a ladder to get to a scaffold platform. Which of these statements is **true**?

 It must be tied and extend either 1 m or five rungs above the platform

 All broken rungs must be clearly marked

 It must be wedged at the bottom to stop it slipping

 Two people must be on the ladder at all times

**14.19** What is the right way to reach the working platform of a mobile access tower?

 Climb up the tower frame on the outside of the tower

 Lean a ladder against the tower and climb up that

 Climb up the ladder built into the tower

 Climb up the outside of the diagonal bracing

D 14

**14.20** A mobile access tower must **not** be used on what surface?

A Soft or uneven ground

B A paved patio

C An asphalt road

D A smooth concrete path

**14.21** What should you do if you need to use a mobile access tower but the brakes don't work?

A Use some wood to wedge the wheels and stop them moving

B Do not use the tower

C Only use the tower if the floor is level

D Get someone to hold the tower while you use it

**14.22** When working in a mobile elevating work platform (MEWP) where should you attach your harness's lanyard?

A To the control box

B To a point on the structure or building you are working on

C To the MEWP handrail

D To the designated anchor point within the platform or basket

**14.23** If you have to work at height in a mobile elevating work platform (MEWP), over or near to deep water, which item of personal protective equipment (PPE) should you wear?

A Wellington boots

B Lifejacket

C Full face respirator

D Full body harness

**14.24** What should you do if you notice your harness or attachment is damaged?

A Stop and tell your supervisor straight away

B Use it and tell your supervisor at the end of the day

C Use a colleague's harness instead

D Stop and tell your supervisor but carry on using it until it is replaced

**14.25** When is it safe to cross a fragile roof?

A If you walk along the line of the bolts

B If you can see fragile roof signs

C If you do not walk on any plastic panels

D If you use crawling boards with handrails

**14.26** What does this sign mean?

A) Load-bearing roof – you can stand on the surface but not on any roof lights

B) Fragile roof – take care when walking on roof surface

C) Fragile roof – do not stand directly on the roof, and use fall protection measures

D) Load-bearing roof – the surface can be slippery when wet

**14.27** What is the **best** way to stop people falling through voids, holes or fragile roof panels?

A) Tell everyone where the dangerous areas are

B) Place secure, load-bearing covers over the dangerous areas and add warning signage

C) Cover the dangerous areas with safety netting and tell everyone to be careful

D) Mark the dangerous areas with red and white warning tape

**14.28** If you are working on a flat roof, what is the **best** way to stop yourself falling over the edge?

A) Put a large warning sign at the edge of the roof

B) Ask someone to watch you and shout when you get too close to the edge

C) Protect the edge with a guard-rail and a toe-board

D) Use red and white tape to mark the edge

**14.29** Who should erect, dismantle or alter a tube and fitting scaffold?

A) Anyone who thinks they can do it

B) Anyone who has the right tools

C) Anyone who is trained, competent and authorised

D) Anyone who is a project manager

**14.30** How do you identify the safe load rating for a scaffold platform?

A) Ask the principal contractor

B) Ask the telehandler driver

C) The safe load is breached when the ledgers start to deflect

D) Refer to the handover certificate or signage

**14.31** If you store materials on a working platform, which statement is **correct**?

A) Materials can be stored unsecured above guard-rail height

B) Materials must be stored so they can't fall and the platform must be able to take their weight

C) Materials can be stored anywhere, even if they pose a trip hazard or block the walkway

D) Materials do not need to be secured if they are going to be there for less than an hour

**14.32** What is the **best** way to stop people being hit by falling tools and materials when you are working above them?

A. Make sure they are wearing safety helmets

B. Tell them you will be working above them and erect signs

C. Exclude people from below the work area with fencing and signs

D. Only allow authorised people underneath the work area

**14.33** If you need to stack materials on a working platform, what is the **best** way to stop them falling over the toe-board?

A. Have brick guards or netting fitted to the edge

B. Put a warning sign on the stack

C. Build the stack so that it leans away from the edge

D. Cover the stack with polythene

# 15 Excavations and confined spaces

**15.01** What **must** happen each time before a shift starts work in an excavation?

- A Someone must go in and sniff the air to see if it is safe
- B A competent person must inspect the excavation
- C A supervisor should stay in the excavation for the first hour
- D A supervisor should watch from the top for the first hour

**15.02** When should an excavation be battered back or stepped?

- A If it is more than 5 m deep
- B If there is water in the bottom of the trench
- C If there is a risk of the sides falling in, regardless of depth
- D If any buried services cross the excavation

**15.03** What do guard-rails around the top of an excavation prevent?

- A Toxic gases collecting in the bottom of the trench
- B People falling into the trench and being injured
- C The sides of the trench collapsing
- D Rainwater running off the ground at the top and into the trench

**15.04** What is the **safest** way to get into and out of a deep excavation?

- A Use an excavator bucket
- B Use the buried services as steps
- C Use the shoring or trench supports
- D Use a fixed staircase

**15.05** What should you do if you see the side supports move when you are working in an excavation?

- A Keep watching to see if they move again
- B Make sure that you and others get out quickly
- C Nothing, as the sides move all the time
- D Work in another part of the excavation

**15.06** Which of the following is the **most** important reason that people should be trained and competent before they are allowed to enter a confined space?

- A Confined spaces never contain breathable air
- B Confined space entrants need to understand the potential hazards
- C Confined spaces are only found on house-building sites
- D Confined spaces always contain flammable or explosive gases

**15.07** Work in a confined space usually needs a risk assessment, a method statement and what other safety document?

A. A permit to enter

B. An up-to-date staff handbook

C. A written contract for the work

D. A company health and safety policy

**15.08** What should you do if your permit to work in a confined space will run out before you finish the task you are carrying out?

A. Carry on working until the job is finished

B. Hand the permit over to the next shift

C. Ask your supervisor to change the date on the permit

D. Make sure that you leave the confined space before the permit runs out

**15.09** What should you do if you have to work in a confined space but there is no rescue team or rescue plan?

A. Assume that a rescue team or plan is not necessary and do the job

B. Get someone to stand at the opening with a rope

C. Do not enter until a rescue plan and team are in place

D. Carry out the job in short spells

**15.10** What is the main reason for having a person positioned immediately outside a confined space whilst work is taking place inside it?

A. To supervise the work inside the confined space

B. To check compliance with the method statement

C. To start the rescue plan if there is an emergency

D. To carry out a risk assessment for the work

**15.11** What is the main cause of people dying while working in a confined space?

A. Presence of methane

B. Lack of oxygen

C. Cold conditions leading to hypothermia

D. Too much oxygen

**15.12** What might happen if the level of oxygen drops below 8% in a confined space?

A. Your hearing could be affected

B. There is a high risk of fire or explosion

C. You could become unconscious

D. You might get dehydrated

**15.13** Before work starts in a confined space, how should the air be checked?

A Someone should go in and sniff the air

B The air should be tested with a monitor

C Someone should look around to see if there is toxic gas

D The air should be tested with a match to see if it stays alight

**15.14** What should you do if you are in a confined space when the gas alarm sounds?

A Switch off the alarm

B Get out of the confined space immediately

C Carry on working but do not use electrical tools

D Carry on working but take plenty of breaks in the fresh air

**15.16** What should you do if you are in a deep trench and you start to feel dizzy?

A Get out, let your head clear and then go back in again

B Carry on working and hope that the feeling will go away

C Make sure that you and any others get out quickly and report it

D Sit down in the trench and take a rest

**15.15** Give **two** reasons why methane gas is dangerous in confined spaces.

Drag your answers into the boxes below

A It can explode

B It makes you hyperactive

C You will not be able to see because of the dense fumes

D It makes you dehydrated

E You may not have enough oxygen to breathe

**15.17** What **three** things should you do before entering a confined space that has sludge at the bottom?

Drag your answers into the boxes below

A. Identify what the sludge is

B. Throw something into the sludge to see how deep it is

C. Put on a disposable face mask

D. Put on respiratory protective equipment (RPE)

E. Have the correct training

**15.18** If you are working in a confined space and notice the smell of bad eggs, what is this a sign of?

A. Hydrogen sulphide

B. Oxygen

C. Methane

D. Carbon dioxide

**15.19** You are in a deep trench. A lorry backs up to the trench and the engine is left running. What should you do?

A. Put on ear defenders to cut out the engine noise

B. Ignore the problem, as the lorry will soon drive away

C. See if there is a toxic gas meter in the trench

D. Get out of the trench quickly

**15.20** When digging, you notice the soil gives off a strange smell. What is this likely to mean?

A. The soil contains a lot of clay

B. The soil has been excavated before

C. The ground has been used to grow crops in the past

D. The ground could be contaminated

**15.21** Which of these is the **most** accurate way to confirm the exact location of buried services?

A. Cable plans

B. Trial holes

C. Survey drawings

D. Architect drawings

**15.22** What equipment **must** you use to hand dig near electrical underground services?

A A jack hammer

B An insulated spade or shovel

C A pick and fork

D An excavator

**15.23** What does it mean if you find a run of coloured marker tape when digging?

A There are buried human remains and you must tell your supervisor

B There is a buried service and further excavation must be carried out with care

C The soil is contaminated and you must wear respiratory protective equipment (RPE)

D The excavation now needs side supports

**15.24** According to the guidance on underground service pipes, what does a yellow service pipe carry?

A Water

B Gas

C Electricity

D Telecoms

**15.25** What should you do if you hit and damage a buried cable when digging?

A Move the cable out of the way and carry on digging

B Wait 10 seconds and then move the cable out of the way

C Do not touch the cable, stop work and report it

D Dig round the cable or dig somewhere else

# E
# Environment

**Contents**

# 16 Environmental awareness and waste control

**16.01** Under environmental law, which statement is **true**?

A) Only directors can be prosecuted if they do not follow the law

B) Only companies can be prosecuted if they do not follow the law

C) Only employees can be prosecuted if they do not follow the law

D) Companies and employees can be prosecuted if they do not follow the law

**16.04** Do you have any responsibility for minimising the amount of waste created?

A) Only if you are told to do so during your site induction

B) Yes, everyone on site has a responsibility to do this

C) No, it is the responsibility of site management

D) Only during the site clean up at the end of the project

**16.02** Which **three** statements are reasons why saving energy is important?

Drag your answers into the boxes below

A) It helps to reduce fuel and energy bills on site

B) It helps to increase energy use on other sites

C) It helps to save natural resources used to generate energy

D) It helps energy companies to charge more for their services

E) It helps to reduce the impact of climate change caused by burning fossil fuels

**16.03** What are **two** of the **best** ways of helping to save energy on site and reduce harmful emissions?

A) Switch off plant and equipment, including generators, when they are not in use

B) Use a generator rather than mains electricity for the offices and small items of equipment

C) Report any defective non-powered hand tools so that they can be repaired or replaced

D) Keep windows and doors closed in offices and welfare facilities when the heating is on

**16.05** Which **two** actions could help minimise waste?

Drag your answers into the boxes below

A Reuse off-cuts (such as half bricks) rather than discarding them

B Use new materials at the beginning of each day

C Leave bags of cement and plaster out in the rain, unprotected

D Only take what you need and return or reseal anything left over

E Always take more than required – just in case you need it

**16.06** Which of the following is bad practice?

A Switching off plant and equipment when it is not in use

B Refuelling carefully to avoid spills

C Storing materials safely

D Mixing all waste in one skip

**16.07** What are the **two**, most important reasons why waste should be segregated on site?

Drag your answers into the boxes below

A The waste will take up less room in a skip

B It is generally more cost effective to dispose of segregated waste

C So the client can check what is being thrown away

D So the wastes can be used or recycled more easily

E To make sure the labourer has enough work to do

**16.08** Which **two** items are classed as hazardous waste?

A Broken bricks

B Untreated timber off-cuts

C Panes of glass

D Fluorescent light tubes

E Used spill kits

**16.09** Which items are hazardous waste and which are non-hazardous waste?

A Fluorescent light tubes

B Broken bricks

C Timber off-cuts

D Oil-based paint

Non-hazardous

Hazardous

**16.10** How should hazardous waste be dealt with on site? Give **two** answers.

Drag your answers into the boxes below

A Segregate it from other waste

B Take it to the nearest Local Authority waste tip

C It can be put in any skip on site

D Place it in the correctly labelled container

E Put it in a mixed waste skip

**16.11**  How should you dispose of a container, or any residue, which has this sign on the label or packaging?

A Put it in any skip or bin

B Follow specific instructions on the label and in the work instructions

C If it is a liquid and less than one litre you can pour it down a drain

D Leave it somewhere for other people to deal with

**16.12** You are on site and need to throw away some waste liquid that has oil in it. What should you do?

A Pour it down a drain or sink in the welfare facilities

B Pour it slowly onto the ground and let it soak away

C Pour it into a sealed container and put it into a general waste skip

D Ask your supervisor what the disposal process is for contaminated water

**16.13** What should you do if there is an oil or diesel spill on site?

A Ignore it – oil or diesel spills do not have serious long-term effects

B Stop work, contain the spill, notify your supervisor and then clean up the spill

C Call the Department for the Environment immediately, so they can arrange to have it cleaned up

D Use a spill kit to clean it up before the end of the day

**16.14** You have been asked to clean up oil that has leaked from machinery onto the ground. What is the right way to do this?

A Put the oily soil into the general waste skip

B Put the oily soil into a separate container for collection as hazardous waste

C Mix the soil up with other soil so that the oil cannot be seen

D Wash the oil away with water and detergent

**16.15** If you notice that a design detail can't be built in the way it has been drawn in the plans, what **two** things should you do?

Drag your answers into the boxes below

A Leave that detail out altogether

B Keep quiet as it will mean more work for you

C Only make the changes when they are approved in writing

D Raise the issue with your supervisor before you start work

E Build it as you think it should be done

E 16

**16.16** Which of the following does **not** cause a nuisance to neighbours of a building site?

A Carefully directed site lighting

B Noise and vibration from construction activities

C Lorries and heavy plant approaching and leaving the site

D Dust and fumes from site

**16.17** You are carrying out a noisy work activity and realise that it cannot be finished within the normal working hours of your site. What is the **first** thing you should do?

A Carry on so that you can finish doing the job as soon as possible

B Stop work and inform site management so they can look at the impact of working hours

C Visit your site's neighbours to tell them what you will be doing

D Ensure you are wearing appropriate hearing protection before you resume work

**16.18** You discover a bird on a nest where you need to work. What should you do?

A Cover it with a bucket

B Move it, do your work and then put it back

C Make others aware of its presence whilst you go and inform your supervisor

D Scare it away

**16.19** You would like to store a pallet of bricks in a space under a tree. What should you do?

A Place them there as they will not be in the way

B Only place them there if they will not be damaged by passing vehicles

C Only place them there if you can avoid damaging the branches or your vehicle

D Do not place them there, as compaction of the soil over the roots can damage the tree

**16.20** What can you do to help protect the environment?

A Arrive for work on time every day

B Keep to the health and safety rules

C Save water and energy wherever possible

D Keep accurate time sheets

**16.21** While excavating you notice some interesting old coins in the loosened soil. What should you do?

A Stop the excavation work and contact your supervisor

B Keep excavating and see how many more you can find

C Hide them. Archaeologists working on site will hold up works

D Keep quiet. You found them so you can keep them

# Congratulations

# You have now completed the core knowledge questions

## For the operatives' test

You still need to prepare for the behavioural case studies, which you can do by:

- watching the film *Setting out* at www.citb.co.uk/settingout
- reading the transcript of the film at the back of this book.

## For the specialists' test

You should now revise the appropriate specialist activity from Section F. You then need to prepare for the behavioural case studies, which you can do by:

- watching the film *Setting out* at www.citb.co.uk/settingout
- reading the transcript of the film at the back of this book.

# F

# Specialist activities

## Contents

If you are preparing for a specialist test you also need to revise the appropriate specialist activity, from those listed below.

# 17 Supervisory

**17.01** When the Construction (Design and Management) Regulations 2015 apply, what **must** be in place before construction work begins?

A The health and safety file

B The construction phase plan

C The method statement

D The construction contract agreement

**17.02** Under the Construction (Design and Management) Regulations 2015, where would you find the arrangements for managing health and safety for the project you are working on?

A In the health and safety file

B In the construction phase plan

C In the contract documentation

D In the designer's risk assessment

**17.03** Under the Construction (Design and Management) Regulations 2015, what **must** be provided before construction work starts, and then maintained until the end of the project?

A A safety log book

B A premises log book

C A car park or other parking facilities

D Adequate welfare facilities

**17.04** Under the Construction (Design and Management) Regulations 2015, which **two** of the following must you ensure workers have received before they start working on site?

A A suitable site induction, specific to the work

B Details of the client's brief and project expectations

C Confirmation of their working hours and rest breaks

D Details of the designer's plan of work

E Information on relevant hazards and control measures

**17.05** How long **must** you keep inspection records under the Construction (Design and Management) Regulations 2015?

A For three months after the inspection has been carried out

B For one week on site before sending them to head office

C Until the construction work is complete and then for three months

D Only until the project is complete

**17.06** Under the Construction (Design and Management) Regulations 2015, when the contractor sets a person to work on a construction site, what **must** they ensure that person has, or be in the process of, obtaining?

A The right skills, knowledge, training and experience

B The relevant competency card

C A hard hat, hi-vis clothing and safety footwear

D A relevant qualification for the work to be undertaken

**17.07** Under the Construction (Design and Management) Regulations 2015, which of the following **must** be in place before demolition work can start?

A) A health and safety file

B) The arrangements for demolition recorded in writing

C) A demolition risk assessment

D) The pre-tender demolition health and safety plan

**17.08** What is the purpose of the health and safety file that is handed to the client at the end of the project?

A) To help people who have to carry out work on the structure in the future

B) To help prepare the final accounts for the structure

C) To record the health and safety standards of the structure

D) To record the accident statistics of the construction project

**17.09** Which piece of equipment is used with a cable avoidance tool (CAT) to detect cables?

A) Compressor

B) Signal generator

C) Metal detector

D) Gas detector

**17.10** In the colour coding of electrical power supplies on site, what voltage does a blue plug represent?

A) 50 volts

B) 110 volts

C) 230 volts

D) 400 volts

**17.11** On the site electrical distribution system, which colour plug indicates a 400 volt supply?

A) Yellow

B) Blue

C) Black

D) Red

**17.12** Why **must** a RCD (residual current device) be used in conjunction with 230 volt electrical equipment?

A) It lowers the voltage

B) It quickly cuts off the power if there is a fault

C) It makes the tool run at a safe speed

D) It saves energy and lowers costs

**17.13** How could a site worker check if the RCD (residual current device) through which a 230 volt hand tool is connected to the supply is working correctly?

A Switch the tool on and off

B Press the test button on the RCD unit

C Switch the power on and off

D Run the tool at top speed to see if it cuts out

**17.14** What should be used to protect passers-by from getting arc eye when electric welding is about to start on your site?

A Warning signs

B Screens

C Personal protective equipment (PPE)

D Nothing

**17.15** Where should an escape route take you to?

A The ground

B The open air

C A place of safety

D A first-aid room

**17.16** Which of the following tasks would you expect the appointed person for first aid to carry out?

A They should provide most of the care normally carried out by a first aider

B They should provide all of the care normally carried out by a first aider

C They should contact the emergency services when required

D They should only apply splints to broken bones

**17.17** What does the proactive monitoring of health and safety procedures involve?

A Ensuring that staff always do the work that they have been instructed to do safely

B Deciding how to prevent accidents similar to those that have already occurred

C Looking at the work to be done, what could go wrong and how it could be done safely

D Checking that all staff read and understand all health and safety notices

**17.18** Why may a young person be more at risk of having an accident?

A Legislation does not apply to anyone under 18 years of age

B They are usually left to work alone to gain experience

C They have less experience and may not recognise danger or understand fully what could go wrong

D They are less likely to wear personal protective equipment (PPE)

**17.19** Which **two** of the following factors must be considered when providing first-aid facilities on site?

Drag your answers into the boxes below

A The cost of first-aid equipment

B The hazards, risks and nature of the work carried out

C The number of people expected to be on site at any one time

D The difficulty in finding time to purchase the necessary equipment

E The space in the site office to store the necessary equipment

**17.20** What regulation contains details of the welfare facilities that **must** be provided on a construction site?

A The Control of Substances Hazardous to Health (COSHH)

B The Construction (Design and Management) Regulations

C The Management of Health and Safety at Work Regulations

D The Workplace (Health, Safety and Welfare) Regulations

**17.21** What does a COSHH assessment tell you?

A How to lift heavy loads and how to protect yourself

B How to work safely in confined spaces

C How to use a substance safely in the environment it is to be used

D How to assess noise levels to protect your hearing

**17.22** You have to use a new substance for the first time and need to carry out a COSHH assessment. What are the **two** main things you will need?

Drag your answers into the boxes below

A Your company's safety policy

B The safety data sheet

C The age of the people doing the work

D The delivery note

E The details of where, who and how you will be using the substance

**17.23** When does an employer have to prepare a written health and safety policy?

A If they employ five people or more

B If they employ three people or more

C If they employ a safety officer

D If the work is going to last more than 30 days

**17.24** If there is a fatal accident or a reportable dangerous occurrence on site, when **must** the Health and Safety Executive (HSE) be informed?

A Immediately

B Within five days

C Within seven days

D Within ten days

**17.25** The significant findings of risk assessments **must** be recorded when how many people are employed?

A Three or more

B Five or more

C Six or more

D Seven or more

**17.26** What **must** happen if a prohibition notice is issued by an inspector of the Health and Safety Executive (HSE) or Local Authority?

A Work can continue, as long as a risk assessment is carried out

B The work that is subject to the notice must stop

C The work can continue if extra safety precautions are taken

D The work in hand can be completed, but no new works started

**17.27** Who should you inform if someone tells you that they have work-related hand-arm vibration syndrome (HAVS)?

A The Health and Safety Executive (HSE)

B The local Health Authority

C The person's doctor

D The nearest hospital

**17.28** In deciding what control measures to take, following a risk assessment that has revealed a risk, what measure should you always consider **first**?

A Make sure personal protective equipment (PPE) is available

B Adapt the work to the individual

C Give priority to measures that protect the whole workforce

D Avoid the risk altogether if possible

**17.29** In considering what measures to take to protect workers against risks to their health and safety, when should personal protective equipment (PPE) be considered?

A First, because it is an effective way to protect people

B First, as the only practical measure

C Never, as using PPE is bad practice

D Only when the risks cannot be eliminated by other means

**17.30** In the context of a risk assessment, what does the term **risk** mean?

A Anything that could cause harm to you or another person

B Any unsafe act or condition which could cause loss, injury or damage

C The likelihood that you, or someone else, could be harmed, and how serious any harm could be

D Any work activity that can be described as hazardous or dangerous

**17.31** From a safety point of view, which of the following should be considered **first** when deciding on the number and location of access and egress points on a site?

A Off road parking for cars and vans

B Access for the emergency services

C Access for heavy vehicles

D Site security

**17.32** What is the purpose of using a permit to work system?

A To ensure that the job is carried out quickly

B To ensure that the job is carried out by the easiest method

C To enable tools and equipment to be properly checked before work starts

D To establish a controlled, safe system of work

**17.33** What is the **best** way for a supervisor or manager to make sure that the operatives doing a job have fully understood a method statement?

A. Put the method statement in a labelled ring-binder in the office

B. Explain the method statement to those doing the job and test their understanding

C. Make sure that those doing the job have read the method statement

D. Display the method statement on a noticeboard in the office

**17.34** Why is it important that hazards are identified?

A. They have the potential to cause injury or harm

B. They must all be eliminated before work can start

C. They must all be notified to the Health and Safety Executive (HSE)

D. So that toolbox talks can be given on the hazards

**17.35** When is it advisable to take precautions to prevent people, plant or materials falling into an excavation?

A. At all times

B. When the excavation is 2 m or more deep

C. When the excavation is 1.2 m or more deep

D. When there is a risk from an underground cable or other service

**17.36** Which of the following precautions should be taken to prevent a dumper that is tipping material into an excavation from falling into it?

A. Dumpers should be kept 5 m away from the excavation

B. Stop blocks should be provided, parallel to the trench and appropriate to the vehicle's wheel size

C. Dumper drivers are required to judge the distance carefully or be given stop signals by another person

D. Cones or signage should be erected to indicate the safe tipping point

**17.37** When planning possible work in a confined space, what should be the **first** consideration?

A. How long the job will take

B. How to avoid the need for operatives to enter the space

C. How many operatives will be required

D. What personal protective equipment (PPE) will be needed

**17.38** Which of the following is a significant hazard when excavating alongside a building or structure?

A. Undermining or weakening the foundations of the building

B. Noise and vibration affecting the occupiers of the building

C. Excavating too deeply into soft ground

D. Damaging the surface finish of the building or structure

**17.39** What danger is created by excessive oxygen in a confined space?

A An increase in the breathing rate of workers

B An increased flammability of combustible materials

C An increased working time inside the work area

D A false sense of security

**17.40** How should cylinders containing liquefied petroleum gas (LPG) be stored on site?

A In a locked cellar with clear warning signs

B In a locked cage at least 3 m from any oxygen cylinders

C In a secure storage container at the back of the site

D Covered by a tarpaulin to shield the compressed cylinder from sunlight

**17.41** Where should liquefied petroleum gas (LPG) cylinders be positioned when supplying an appliance in a site cabin?

A Inside the cabin in a locked cupboard

B Under the cabin

C Inside the cabin next to the appliance

D Outside the cabin

**17.42** What should be the capacity of a spillage bund around a fuel storage tank, in addition to the volume of the tank?

A 10% (110% of the total content)

B 30% (130% of the total content)

C 50% (150% of the total content)

D 75% (175% of the total content)

**17.43** Which of the following should be the **first** consideration if you need to use a hazardous substance?

A What instruction, training and supervision to provide

B What health surveillance arrangements will be needed

C How to minimise risk and control exposure

D How to monitor the exposure of workers in the workplace

**17.44** Before allowing a lifting operation to be carried out, where should you ensure that the sequence of operations is recorded to enable a safe lift?

A In the crane hire contract

B In an approved lifting plan or method statement

C In a lifting operation toolbox talk

D In a risk assessment

**17.45** Where **must** the number of people who may be carried in a passenger hoist on site be displayed?

A. On a legible notice in the site welfare area

B. On a legible notice within the cage of the hoist

C. On a legible notice displayed during the site induction

D. On a legible notice handed to the hoist operator

**17.46** How should access be controlled if people are working in a riser shaft?

A. By a site security operative

B. By those who are working in it

C. By the main contractor

D. By a permit to work system

**17.47** What is regarded as the **last resort** in the hierarchy of control for operatives' safety when working at height?

A. Safety harness

B. Mobile elevating work platform (MEWP)

C. Mobile access tower

D. Access tower scaffold

**17.48** When do the Work at Height Regulations require a working platform to be inspected by a competent person?

A. After it has been erected and then at monthly intervals

B. After it has been erected and then at intervals not exceeding 10 days

C. Only after it has been erected

D. After it has been erected and then at intervals not exceeding seven days

**17.49** What is the advantage of using safety nets rather than a harness and fall-arrest lanyard?

A. Safety nets do not need inspecting

B. Workers' lanyards can get entangled with other workers' lanyards

C. Safety nets provide collective fall protection

D. Safety nets can be rigged by anyone

**17.50** What should be included in a method statement for working at height? Give **three** answers.

Drag your answers into the boxes below

A The cost of the job and the time it will take

B The sequence of operations and the equipment to be used

C How much insurance cover will be required

D How falls are to be prevented

E Who will supervise the job on site

**17.51** When putting people to work above public areas, what should be your **first** consideration?

A To minimise the number of people below at any one time

B To prevent complaints from the public

C To let the public know what you are doing

D To prevent anything falling onto people below

**17.52** What **must** edge protection be designed to do?

A Allow persons to work on both sides of it

B Secure tools and materials close to the edge

C Warn people where the edge of the roof is

D Prevent people and materials from falling

**17.53** The Beaufort Scale is important when working at height externally. What does it measure?

A It measures air temperature

B It measures the load-bearing capacity of a flat roof

C It measures wind speed

D It measures the load-bearing capacity of a scaffold

**17.54** Why is it dangerous to use inflatable airbags for fall arrest if they are too big for the area to be protected?

A They will exert a sideways pressure on anything that is containing them

B The pressure in the bags will cause them to burst

C The inflation pump will become overloaded

D They will not fully inflate

**17.55** If a scaffold is **not** complete, which of the following actions should be taken by the supervisor?

A Make sure that the scaffolders complete the scaffold

B Tell operatives not to use the scaffold

C Display a warning notice and tell operatives to use the scaffold with care

D Prevent access to the scaffold and add warning signage

**17.56** Following a scaffold inspection under the Work at Height Regulations, how soon **must** a report be given to the person on whose behalf the inspection was made?

A Within two hours

B Within six hours

C Within 12 hours

D Within 24 hours

**17.58** On a scaffold, what **must** be the largest unprotected gap between any guard-rail, toe-board, barrier or other similar means of protection?

A 400 mm

B 470 mm

C 500 mm

D 600 mm

**17.57** What is the **minimum** height of the main guard-rail on a scaffold?

**17.59** What is the **maximum** unprotected gap allowed between any guard-rail, toe-board, barrier or other similar means of protection on a scaffold?

400 mm    470 mm    500 mm    600 mm

**17.60** Which of the following is a fall-arrest system?

A Guard-rail and toe-board

B Mobile access tower

C Mobile elevating work platform (MEWP)

D Safety harness and lanyard

**17.61** Under the requirements of the Work at Height Regulations, what must the **minimum** width of a working platform be?

A Suitable and sufficient for the job in hand

B Two scaffold boards wide

C Three scaffold boards wide

D Four scaffold boards wide

**17.62** What is the **maximum** vertical height that a fixed ladder can be climbed, before an intermediate landing place is required?

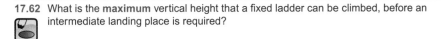

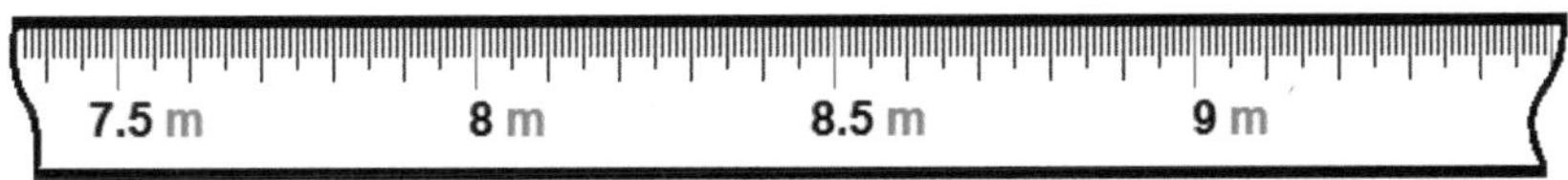

**17.63** What should you do if you notice that operatives working above a safety net are dropping off-cuts of material and other debris into the net?

A Nothing, as the debris is all collecting in one place

B Ensure that the net is cleared of debris weekly

C Have the net cleared and inspected, then ensure it is not allowed to happen again

D Ensure that the net is cleared of debris daily

**17.64** Ideally, where should a safety net be rigged?

A Immediately below where you are working

B 2 m below where you are working

C 6 m below where you are working

D At any height below the working position

**17.65** What is the **main** danger of leaving someone who has fallen suspended in a harness for too long?

A The anchorage point may fail

B They may try to climb back up the structure and fall again

C They may suffer loss of consciousness or fatal injury

D It is a distraction for other workers

**17.66** When should guard-rails be fitted to a working platform?

A If it is possible to fall 2 m

B At any height if a fall could result in an injury

C If it is possible to fall 3 m

D Only if materials are being stored on the working platform

**17.67** A design feature of some airbags used for fall arrest is a controlled leak rate. If you are using these, what **must** you ensure about the inflation pump?

A It must be electrically powered

B It must be switched off from time to time to avoid over-inflation

C It must run all the time while work is carried out at height

D It must be switched off when the airbags are full

**17.68** What is your **least** reliable source of information when assessing the level of vibration from a powered, hand tool?

A In-use vibration measurement of the tool

B Vibration figures taken from the tool manufacturer's handbook

C Your own judgement based upon observation or experience

D Vibration data from the Health and Safety Executive's (HSE) master list

**17.69** What does the term **lower exposure action value** (80 decibels (dBA)) mean, when referring to noise?

A The average background noise level

B The noise level at which the worker can request hearing protection

C The level of noise which must not be exceeded on the site boundary

D The noise level at which the worker must wear hearing protection

**17.70** At what decibel (dBA) level does it become mandatory for an employer to establish hearing protection zones?

A 80 decibels (dBA)

B 85 decibels (dBA)

C 90 decibels (dBA)

D 95 decibels (dBA)

**17.71** At what **minimum** noise level **must** you provide hearing protection to workers if they ask for it?

A 80 decibels (dBA)

B 85 decibels (dBA)

C 87 decibels (dBA)

D 90 decibels (dBA)

**17.72** What is the significance of a weekly or daily personal noise exposure of 87 decibels (dBA)?

A It is the lower action value and no action is necessary

B It is the upper action value and hearing protection must be issued

C It is the peak sound pressure and all work must stop

D It is the exposure limit value and must not be exceeded

**17.73** If a heavy load has been delivered to site, what is the **first** thing that should be considered before trying to move it?

A How far the load would have to be carried manually

B How the risk of manual handling could be reduced

C How many people are needed to lift the load

D How the need to manually lift the load could be avoided

# 18 Demolition

**18.01** If asbestos is present what should happen before demolition or refurbishment takes place?

A Advise workers that asbestos is present, then continue with the demolition

B Remove all asbestos as far as is reasonably practicable

C Advise the Health and Safety Executive (HSE) that asbestos is present, then continue with the demolition

D Inspect the condition of the asbestos materials

**18.02** What kind of survey is required to identify asbestos prior to demolition?

A Type 3 survey

B Management survey

C Demolition survey

D Type 2 survey

**18.03** Who **must** be the **first** person a demolition contractor appoints before undertaking demolition operations?

A A competent person to supervise the work

B A sub-contractor to strip out the buildings

C A safety officer to check on health and safety compliance

D A quantity surveyor to price the extras

**18.04** If there are any doubts about a building's stability, who should a demolition contractor consult?

A Another demolition contractor

B A structural engineer

C A Health and Safety Executive (HSE) factory inspector

D The company safety adviser

**18.05** Which piece of equipment could a 17-year-old trainee demolition operative use unsupervised?

A Excavator 360°

B Dump truck

C Wheelbarrow

D Rough terrain forklift

**18.06** When would it be unsafe to operate a scissor lift?

A If the controls on the platform are used

B If the ground is soft and sloping

C If weather protection is not fitted

D If the machine only has half a tank of fuel

**18.07** On site, what is the **minimum** distance that oxygen should be stored away from propane, butane or any other gas?

1 m 2 m 3 m 4 m

**18.08** Where should liquefied petroleum gas (LPG) cylinders be located when being used for heating or cooking in site cabins?

A Under the kitchen work surface

B Inside but near the door for ventilation

C In a nearby storage container

D Securely outside the cabin

**18.09** What type of fire extinguisher should **not** be provided where petrol or diesel is being stored?

A Foam

B Water

C Dry powder

D Carbon dioxide

**18.10** What is **most** likely to be caused by continual use of hand-held breakers or drills?

A Dermatitis

B Weil's disease (leptospirosis)

C Vibration white finger

D Skin cancer

**18.11** What is the **most** common source of high levels of lead in the blood of operatives during demolition work of an old building?

A Stripping lead sheeting

B Cold cutting lead-covered cable

C Cold cutting fuel tanks

D Hot cutting coated steel

**18.12** Which of the following items of personal protective equipment (PPE) provides the lowest level of protection when working in dusty conditions?

A Dust mask

B Positive pressure-powered respirator

C FFP3-rated half mask respirator

D Self-contained breathing apparatus

**18.13** Which of the following would be suitable to use when cutting coated steelwork?

A A disposable dust mask

B A positive pressure-powered respirator

C A high-efficiency dust respirator

D A nuisance dust mask

**18.14** Where is the **only** place you will **not** find information about the daily checks required for mobile plant?

A On stickers attached to the machine

B In the manufacturer's handbook

C In the supplier's information

D On the health and safety law poster

**18.15** What should you do while reversing mobile plant if you lose sight of the vehicle marshaller who is directing you?

A Carry on reversing slowly

B Stop the vehicle

C Adjust your wing mirror

D Sound the horn and move forward

**18.16** What should you do when leaving mobile plant unattended?

A Leave the engine running, if safe to do so

B Park it in a safe place, remove the keys and lock it

C Put the parking brake on and tell people not to use it

D Put a sign saying 'no unauthorised access' on it

**18.17** Which statement is **true** with regard to using machines?

A Guards can be removed to make work easier

B It's OK to wear rings and other jewellery as long as you take care

C You can carefully remove waste material while the machine is in motion

D Never use a machine unless you have been trained and given permission to use it

**18.18** Which of the following is **not** part of a plant operator's daily pre-use check?

A Emergency systems

B Engine oil level

C Hydraulic fluid level

D Brake pad wear

**18.19** Which of these statements is **true** in relation to an operator of a scissor lift?

A They must be trained and authorised in the use of the equipment

B They must only use the ground level controls

C They must be in charge of the work team

D They must ensure that only one person is on the platform at any time

**18.20** On demolition sites, what **must** the drivers of plant have, for their own and others' safety?

A Adequate visibility from the driving position

B A temperature controlled cab

C Wet weather gear for when it's raining

D A supervisor in the cab with them

**18.21** When **must** head and tail lights be used on mobile plant?

A If the plant is using the same traffic route as private cars

B When the plant is operating in conditions of poor visibility

C When the plant is operated by a trainee

D Only if the plant is crossing pedestrian routes

**18.22** What safety feature is provided by FOPS on mobile plant?

A The speed is limited when tracking over hard surfaces

B The machine stops automatically if the operator lets go of the controls

C The operator is protected from falling objects

D The reach is limited when working near to live overhead cables

**18.23** What should you do if you discover underground services **not** previously identified?

A Fill in the hole immediately

B Stop work until the situation has been resolved

C Cut the pipe or cable to see if it's live

D Get the machine driver to dig it out

**18.24** What action should you take if you discover unlabelled drums or containers on site?

A Put them in the nearest waste skip

B Ignore them, as they will get flattened during the demolition

C Stop work until they have been safely dealt with

D Open them and smell the contents to see if they are flammable

**18.25** If the plant you are driving has defective brakes, what action should you take?

A Reduce your speed

B Report it and carry on working

C Report it and isolate the machine

D Use the handbrake instead of the foot brake

**18.26** What action should be taken if a wire rope sling is defective?

A Do not use it and make sure that no-one else can

B Only use it for up to half of its safe working load

C Report the defect at the end of the day

D Only use it for small lifts under 1 tonne

**18.27** Which **two** of the following documents refer to the specific hazards associated with demolition work in confined spaces?

A Safety policy

B Permit to work

C Risk assessment

D Scaffolding permit

E Hot-work permit

**18.28** When asbestos material is suspected in buildings to be demolished, what is the **first** priority?

A Ensure a competent person carries out an asbestos survey

B Notify the Health and Safety Executive (HSE) of the possible presence of asbestos

C Remove and dispose of the asbestos

D Employ a licensed asbestos remover

**18.29** What is the **safest** method of demolishing brick or internal walls by hand?

A Undercut the wall at ground level

B Work across in even courses from the ceiling down

C Work from the doorway at full height

D Cut down at corners and collapse in sections

**18.30** Who should be consulted before demolition is carried out near to overhead cables?

A) The Health and Safety Executive (HSE)

B) The fire service

C) The electricity supply company

D) The land owner

**18.31** When demolishing a building in controlled sections, what is the **most** important consideration for the remaining structure?

A) The soft strip is completed

B) All non-ferrous metals are removed

C) It remains stable

D) Trespassers cannot get in at night

**18.32** Where would you find out the method for controlling identified hazards on a demolition project?

A) The demolition toolbox

B) The health and safety file

C) The pre-tender health and safety plan

D) The construction phase plan

**18.33** How **must** cans or drums be stored, to prevent any leakage from spreading?

A) On wooden pallets off the ground

B) On their sides and chocked to prevent movement

C) Upside down to prevent water penetrating the screw top

D) In a bund

**18.34** What safety devices should be fitted between the pipes and the gauges of oxy-propane cutting equipment?

A) Non-return valves

B) On-off taps

C) Flame retardant tape

D) Flashback arresters

**18.35** With regard to the safe method of working, what is the **most** important subject of induction training for demolition operatives?

A) Working hours on the site

B) Explanation of the method statement

C) Location of welfare facilities

D) COSHH assessments

**18.36** What should be obtained before carrying out the demolition cutting of fuel tanks?

A A gas free certificate

B An isolation certificate

C A risk assessment

D A COSHH assessment

**18.37** What do the letters SWL stand for?

A Satisfactory working limit

B Safe working level

C Satisfactory weight limit

D Safe working load

**18.38** Which of the following is **true** in relation to the safe working load of a piece of equipment?

A It must never be exceeded

B It is a guide figure that may be exceeded slightly

C It may be exceeded by 10% only

D It gives half the maximum weight to be lifted

**18.39** What should be clearly marked on all lifting gear?

A Date of manufacture

B Name of maker

C Date next test is due

D Safe working load

**18.40** How often should lifting accessories be thoroughly examined?

A Every three months

B Every six months

C Every 14 months

D Every 18 months

**18.41** What is the correct way to climb off a machine?

A Jump down from the seated position

B Climb down, facing forward

C Climb down, facing the machine

D Use a ladder

**18.42** When is it acceptable to carry passengers on a machine?

A When the employer gives permission

B When they are carried in the skip

C When the machine is fitted with a purpose-made passenger seat

D When the maximum speed is no greater than 10 mph

# 19 Highway works

**19.01** Why is it **not** safe to use diesel to prevent asphalt sticking to the bed of lorries?

A It will create a slipping hazard

B It will corrode the bed of the lorry

C It will create an environmental hazard

D It will react with the asphalt, creating explosive fumes

**19.02** You are moving or laying slabs, paving blocks or kerbs on site. Which **two** of the following methods would be classed as manual handling?

A Using a scissor lifter attachment on an excavator

B Using a trolley or sack barrow

C Using a suction lifter attached to an excavator

D Using a two man scissor lifter

E Using a crane with fork attachment

**19.03** What are **two** effects of under-inflated tyres on the operation of a machine?

A It decreases the operating speed of the engine

B It can make the machine unstable

C It causes increased tyre wear

D It causes decreased tyre wear

E It increases the operating speed of the engine

**19.04** If you are driving any plant that may overturn, when **must** a seat belt be worn?

A When travelling over rough ground

B When the vehicle is loaded

C When you are carrying passengers

D At all times

**19.05** If the dead man's handle on a machine does **not** operate, what should you do?

A Keep quiet in case you get the blame

B Report it at the end of the shift

C Try and fix it or repair it yourself

D Stop and report it immediately to your supervisor

**19.06** When can you carry authorised passengers in vehicles?

A Only if your supervisor gives you permission

B Only if a suitable secure seat is provided for each of them

C Only when off the public highway

D Only if you have a full driving licence

**19.07** When it is necessary to tip into an excavation, what is the preferred method of preventing the vehicle getting too close to the edge?

A Signage

B Driver's experience

C Signaller

D Stop blocks

**19.08** Which of these is the **safest** method of operating a machine under electrical power lines when it has an extending jib or boom?

A Erect signs to warn drivers while they are operating the machines

B Adapt the machine to limit the extension of the jib or boom

C Place a warning notice on the machine

D Let down the tyres on the machine to increase the clearance

**19.09** When using lifting equipment, such as a cherry picker, lorry loader or excavator, how should you follow the indicated safe working load?

A It must never be exceeded

B It is a guide figure that may be exceeded slightly

C It may be exceeded by 10% only

D It gives half the maximum weight to be lifted

**19.10** Which checks should the operator of a mobile elevating work platform (MEWP) (for example, a cherry picker) carry out before using it?

A That a seat belt is provided for the operator

B That a roll-over cage is fitted

C That the hydraulic system is drained

D That emergency systems operate correctly

**19.11** A single vehicle is being used to carry out mobile highway works during the day. What sign or symbol **must** be clearly displayed on or at the rear of the vehicle?

A A road narrows sign (left or right)

B A specific task warning sign (for example, gully cleaning)

C A keep left or right arrow

D A roadworks ahead sign

**19.12** When should you switch on the amber flashing beacon fitted to your highways vehicle?

A At all times

B When travelling to and from the depot

C When it is being used as a works vehicle

D Only in poor visibility

**19.13** What **must** you do approximately 200 m before a site works access on a motorway?

A Switch on the vehicle hazard lights

B Switch on the flashing amber beacon

C Switch on the headlights

D Switch on the flashing amber beacon and the appropriate indicator

**19.14** How often **must** a competent person thoroughly examine lifting equipment for lifting persons (for example, a cherry picker)?

A Every six months

B Every 12 months

C Every 18 months

D Every 24 months

**19.15** What **must** you do before towing a trailer fitted with independent brakes?

A Fit a safety chain

B Fit a cable that applies the trailer's brakes if the tow hitch fails

C Use a rope to secure the trailer to the tow hitch

D Make sure it is possible to drive at a maximum speed of 25 mph along the route you have chosen

**19.16** What **must** you do when getting off plant and vehicles?

A Use a pair of steps which allow you to climb out of the vehicle

B Use the wheels and tyres for access

C Use the designated access and egress point whilst maintaining three points of contact with the vehicle

D Look before you jump, then jump down facing the vehicle

**19.17** What should you do when leaving plant unattended?

A Leave the amber flashing beacon on

B Apply the brake, switch off the engine and remove the key

C Leave it in a safe place with the engine ticking over

D Park with blocks under the front wheels

**19.18** What **must** you have before towing a compressor on the highway? Give **two** answers.

A Permission from your supervisor

B The correct class of driving licence

C Permission from the police

D Permission from the compressor hire company

E Working lights, and a number plate on the compressor that matches that of the towing vehicle

**19.19** Who is responsible for the security of the load on a vehicle?

A The driver's supervisor

B The police

C The driver

D The driver's company

**19.20** What is the correct way to dismount from the cab or driving seat of plant and vehicles?

A Use three points of contact facing forwards (away from the vehicle)

B Jump down facing forwards (away from the vehicle)

C Use three points of contact facing backwards (towards the vehicle)

D Jump down well clear of the vehicle

**19.21** Why is it necessary to wear hi-vis clothing when working on roads?

A So road users and plant operators can see you

B So your supervisor can see you

C To protect clothes worn underneath from damage

D Because it will keep you warm

**19.22** You are working on a dual carriageway with a 60 mph speed limit although you are not in the working space. What is the **minimum** standard of hi-vis clothing that you **must** wear?

A Reflective waistcoat

B Reflective long-sleeved jacket

C Reflective sash

D Reflective hard hat

**19.23** When kerbing works are being carried out, how should kerbs be taken off the vehicle?

A By lifting them off manually using the correct technique

B By pushing them off the back

C By using mechanical means, such as a machine fitted with a grab

D By asking your workmate to give you a hand

**19.24** What is the purpose of an on-site risk assessment?

A To ensure there is no risk of traffic build-up due to the works in progress

B To identify hazards and risks specific to the site in order to ensure a safe system of work

C To ensure that the work can be carried out in reasonable safety

D To protect the employer from prosecution

**19.25** In which **two** places would you find information about the distances for setting out highways signs in advance of the works under different road conditions?

A In the Traffic Signs Manual (Chapter 8)

B In the Pink Book

C On the back of the sign

D In the Works Order

E In the new Code of Practice (Red Book)

**19.26** What should you do if you are the driver of a vehicle and lose sight of the vehicle marshaller while reversing your vehicle?

A Continue reversing slowly

B Continue reversing, as long as your vehicle is equipped with a klaxon and flashing lights

C Stop and locate the vehicle marshaller

D Find someone else to watch you reverse safely

**19.27** What should you do with materials that have to be kept on site overnight?

A Don't stack them above 2 m high

B Stack them safely and in a secure area

C Put pins and bunting around them

D Only stack them on the grass verge

**19.28** When providing portable traffic signals on roads used by cyclists, what action should you take?

A Locate the signals at bends in the road

B Allow more time for slow-moving traffic by increasing the all-red phase of the signals

C Operate the signals manually

D Use stop-and-go boards only

**19.29** What is the **main** reason why temporary highways signing needs to be removed when works are completed?

A It gets traffic flowing

B It is a legal requirement

C To allow the road to be opened fully

D To reuse signs on new jobs

**19.30** When should installed highways signs and guarding equipment be inspected?

A Immediately after it has been used

B No more frequently than once a week

C Every hour, except when the site is unattended

D Regularly, and at least once every day, including when the site is unattended

F 19

**19.31** Which **two** site conditions must be met before traffic management can be reduced to the **minimum** requirements?

A Traffic is heavy

B Visibility is good

C There are double yellow lines

D There is a footpath

E It is a period of low risk

**19.32** What traffic management is required when carrying out a maintenance job on a motorway?

A The same as would be required on a single carriageway

B A flashing beacon and a keep left or right sign

C A scheme installed by a registered traffic management contractor

D Ten 1 m high cones and a 1 m high 'men working' sign

**19.33** What is the **minimum** traffic management required when carrying out a short-term minor maintenance job in a quiet, low-speed side road?

A A flashing amber beacon and a keep left or right arrow

B The same as required for a road excavation

C Five cones and a blue arrow

D Temporary traffic lights

**19.34** What is the **maximum** distance between the 'roadworks ahead' signs for work activities that move along the carriageway, such as sweeping, verge mowing and road lining?

A Quarter of a mile

B Half a mile

C One mile

D Two miles

**19.35** What action is required when a highways vehicle fitted with a direction arrow is travelling from site to site?

A Point the direction arrow up

B Travel slowly from site to site

C Point the direction arrow down

D Cover or remove the direction arrow

**19.36** How **must** signs on footways be located?

A So that they block the footway

B So that they can be read by site personnel

C So that they do not create a hazard for pedestrians

D So that they can be easily removed

**19.37** What should you do if drivers approaching highway works **cannot** see the advance signs clearly because of poor visibility or obstructions caused by road features?

A Place additional signs in advance of the works

B Extend the safety zones

C Extend the sideways clearance

D Lengthen the lead-in taper

**19.38** How should you protect a portable traffic-light cable that crosses a road?

A It should be secured firmly to the road surface

B A cable crossing protector must be used with ramp warning signs

C It can be unprotected if it is less than 10 mm in diameter

D It should be placed in a slot cut into the road surface

**19.39** What action is required where passing traffic may block the view of highways signs?

A Signs must be larger

B Signs must be duplicated on both sides of the road

C Signs must be placed higher

D Additional signs must be placed in advance of the works

**19.40** How **must** highway signs, lights and guarding equipment be properly secured?

A By built-in weights where possible

B By roping them to concrete blocks or kerb stones

C By pushing them securely into the soft verge

D By iron weights suspended from the frame by chains or other strong material

**19.41** Which is **not** an approved means of controlling traffic at roadworks?

A Priority signs

B Police supervision

C Hand signals by operatives

D A give-and-take system

**19.42** What action is required if a vehicle detector on temporary traffic lights becomes defective?

A Control traffic at the defective end using hand signals

B Operate on all-red and call the service engineer

C Operate on fixed time or manual and call the service engineer

D Switch the lights off until the supervisor arrives on site

**19.43** How should portable traffic signals be assembled and placed?

A As speedily as possible

B In an organised manner, to a specified sequence

C During the night

D As work starts each morning

**19.44** What action is required where it is **not** possible to maintain the correct safety zone?

A Barrier off the working space

B Place additional advance signing

C Use extra cones on the lead-in taper

D Stop work and consult your supervisor

**19.45** In which of the following circumstances can someone enter the safety zone?

A To store unused plant

B To maintain cones and signs

C To park site vehicles

D To store materials

**19.46** What action should you take if a vehicle, driven by a member of the public, enters the coned off area on a dual carriageway?

A Remove a cone and direct the driver back on to the live carriageway

B Ignore them

C Shout and wave them off site

D Help them to leave the site safely using the nearest designated exit

**19.47** When working after dark, is mobile plant exempt from the requirement to show lights?

A Yes, always

B Yes, if authorised by the supervisor

C Only if they are not fitted to the machine as standard

D Not in any circumstances

**19.48** What is the purpose of the safety zone?

A To indicate the works area

B To protect you from the traffic and the traffic from you

C To allow extra working space in an emergency

D To give a safe route around the working area

**19.49** What should be used to protect the public from a shallow excavation in a public footway?

A Pins and bunting

B Nothing

C Cones

D Barriers with tapping rails

**19.50** In which of the following circumstances would it **not** be safe to use a cherry picker for working at height?

A When a roll-over cage is not fitted

B When the ground is uneven and sloping

C When weather protection is not fitted

D When the operator is clipped to an anchorage point in the basket

**19.51** Where would you find information about working on a dual carriageway with a speed limit above 40 mph?

A In the welfare cabin

B In the Blue Book

C In the Traffic Signs Manual (Chapter 8)

D In the Pink Book

**19.52** What is **not** usually something to consider while undertaking a site-specific risk assessment before starting highway works?

A The cost of the sub-contractor who will be carrying out the work

B The amount and type of traffic

C The effect of different weather conditions

D The type and size of the road

# 20 Specialist work at height

**20.01** If you need to store materials on a roof, what **three** things **must** you do?

- A Check the load bearing capability of the roof to avoid damage to the structure
- B Stack materials no more than 1.2 m above the guard-rail height
- C Ensure there is safe access and clear working areas around the materials for everyone working on the roof
- D Use a gin wheel and rope tied to a temporary tripod at the roof edge for raising and lowering the materials
- E Store the materials in a way that prevents them from falling off, or being blown off, the roof

**20.02** What should you do if a safety lanyard has damaged stitching?

- A Use the lanyard if the damaged stitching is less than 5 cm long
- B Get a replacement lanyard before starting work
- C Not use the damaged lanyard and work without one
- D Use the lanyard if the damaged stitching is less than 15 cm long

**20.03** What is the **main** danger of leaving someone who has fallen suspended in a harness for too long?

- A The anchorage point may fail
- B They may try to climb back up the structure and fall again
- C They may suffer loss of consciousness or fatal injury
- D It is a distraction for other workers

**20.04** If using inflatable airbags as a means of fall arrest, what **must** you ensure with regard to the inflation pump?

- A It must be electrically powered
- B It must be switched off from time to time to avoid over-inflation
- C It must run all the time while work is carried out at height
- D It must be switched off when the airbags are full

**20.05** Why is it dangerous to use inflatable airbags that are too big for the area to be protected?

- A They will exert a sideways pressure on anything that is containing them
- B The pressure in the bags will cause them to burst
- C The inflation pump will become overloaded
- D They will not fully inflate

**20.06** When is it **most** appropriate to use a safety harness and lanyard for working at height?

- A Only when the roof has a steep pitch
- B Only when crossing a flat roof with clear roof lights
- C Only when all other options for fall prevention have been ruled out
- D Only when materials are stored at height

**20.07** When trying to clip your lanyard to an anchor point you find the locking device does **not** work. What should you do?

A Carry on working and report it later

B Tie the lanyard in a knot round the anchor

C Stop work and report it to your supervisor

D Carry on working without it

**20.08** What is the **main** reason for using a safety net or other soft-landing system rather than a personal fall-arrest system?

A Soft-landing systems are cheaper to use and do not need inspecting

B It is always easier to rescue workers who fall into a soft-landing system

C Specialist training is not required to install soft-landing systems

D Soft-landing systems are collective fall arrest measures

**20.09** What is the **maximum** permitted gap between the guard-rails on a working platform?

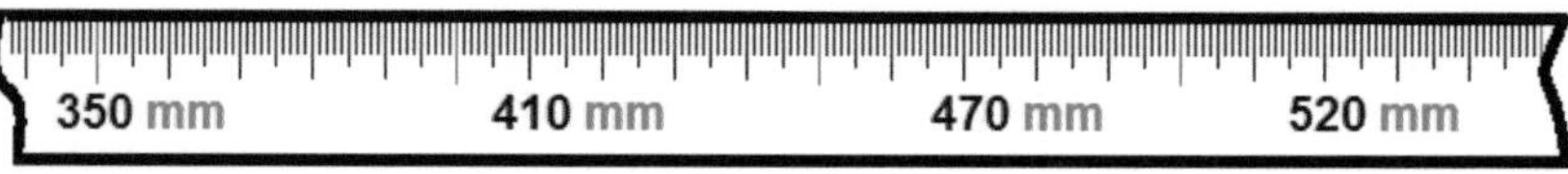


**20.10** What is edge protection designed to do?

A Make access to the roof easier

B Secure tools and materials close to the edge

C Stop rainwater running off the roof onto workers below

D Prevent people and materials from falling

**20.11** When should guard-rails be fitted to a working platform?

A If it is possible to fall 2 m

B At any height if a fall could result in an injury

C If it is possible to fall 3 m

D Only if materials are being stored on the working platform

**20.12** The Beaufort Scale is important when working at height externally. What does it measure?

A It measures air temperature

B It measures the load-bearing capacity of a flat roof

C It measures wind speed

D It measures the load-bearing capacity of a scaffold

**20.13** Before starting work at height, the weather forecast says the wind will increase to Force 7. What is the **best** description of the wind conditions?

A A moderate breeze that can raise light objects, such as dust and leaves

B A near gale that will make it difficult to move about and handle materials

C A gentle breeze that you can feel on your face

D Hurricane winds that will uproot trees and cause structural damage

**20.14** If you have to lean over an exposed edge while working at height, how should you wear your safety helmet?

A Tilted back on your head so that it doesn't fall off

B Take your helmet off while leaning over then put it on again afterwards

C Wear the helmet as usual but use the chinstrap

D Wear the helmet back to front whilst leaning over

**20.15** Before climbing a ladder you notice that it has a rung missing near the top. What should you do?

A Do not use the ladder and immediately report the defect

B Use the ladder but take care when stepping over the position of the missing rung

C Turn the ladder over so that the missing rung is near the bottom and then use it

D See if you can find a piece of wood to replace the rung

**20.16** How far should a ladder extend above the stepping-off point if there is no alternative, firm handhold?

A Three rungs

B Two rungs

C One metre

D Half a metre

**20.17** When using portable or pole ladders for access, what is the **maximum** vertical distance between landings?

A There is no maximum

B 4 m

C 9 m

D 30 m

**20.18** You need to use a ladder to access a roof but the only place to rest the ladder is on a run of plastic gutter. What **two** things should you consider doing?

A Resting the ladder on a gutter support bracket

B Resting the ladder against the gutter, climbing it and quickly tying it off

C Finding another way to access the roof

D Using a proprietary stand-off device that allows the ladder to rest against the wall

E Positioning the ladder at a shallow angle so that it rests below the gutter

**20.19** Who should erect and dismantle scaffold towers?

A Someone who has the instruction book

B Someone who is trained, competent and authorised

C Advanced scaffolders

D Someone who has worked on them before

**20.20** What is the recommended **maximum** height for a free-standing mobile tower when it is used indoors?

A There is no restriction

B Three lifts

C The height recommended by the manufacturer

D Three times the longest base dimension

**20.21** After gaining access to the platform of a correctly erected mobile access tower, what is the **first** thing you should do?

A Check that the tower's brakes are locked on

B Check for overhead power lines

C Close the access hatch to stop people or equipment from falling

D Check that the tower does not rock or wobble

**20.22** What **must** you do before a mobile access tower is moved?

A Clear the platform of people and equipment

B Get a permit to work

C Get approval from the principal contractor

D Make arrangements with the forklift truck driver

**20.23** An outdoor tower scaffold has stood overnight in high winds and heavy rain. What should you ensure before the scaffold is used?

A That the brakes still work

B That the scaffold is tied to the adjacent structure

C That the scaffold is inspected by a competent person

D That the platform hatch still works correctly

**20.24** What should someone working from a cherry picker attach their lanyard to?

A A strong part of the structure that they are working on

B A secure anchorage point inside the platform

C A secure point on the boom of the machine

D A scaffold guard-rail

**20.25** You are working at height from a cherry picker when the weather becomes very windy. What should your **first** consideration be?

A Tie all lightweight objects to the handrails of the basket

B Clip your lanyard to the structure that you are working on

C Tie the cherry picker basket to the structure you are working on

D Decide whether the machine will remain stable

**20.26** If you are on a cherry picker but it does not quite reach where you need to work, what should you do?

A Use a stepladder balanced on the machine platform

B Extend the machine fully and stand on the guard-rails

C Abandon the machine and use a long extending ladder

D Do not carry out the job until you have an alternative means of access

**20.27** If you are working at height and operating a mobile elevating work platform (MEWP), when is it acceptable for someone to use the ground-level controls?

A If the person on the ground is trained and you are not

B In an emergency

C If you need to jump off the MEWP to gain access to the work

D If you need both hands free to carry out the job

**20.28** When is it acceptable to jump off a mobile elevating work platform (MEWP) on to a high level work platform?

A If the work platform is fitted with edge protection

B If the machine operator stays in the basket

C Not under any circumstances

D If the machine is being operated from the ground-level controls

**20.29** How will you know the **maximum** weight or number of people that can be lifted safely on a mobile elevating work platform (MEWP)?

A The weight limit is reached when the platform is full

B It will be stated on the health and safety law poster

C You will be told during site induction

D It will be stated on an information plate fixed to the machine

**20.30** When is it safe to use a mobile elevating work platform (MEWP) on soft ground?

A When the ground is dry

B When the machine can stand on scaffold planks laid over the soft ground

C When ground load bearing capacity has been assessed as suitable

D Never

**20.31** If you need to cross a fragile roof, how do you establish if it is fragile?

A Tread gently and listen for cracking

B Stop and seek advice

C Look at the roof surface and make your own assessment

D It does not matter if you walk along a line of bolts

**20.32** If you notice some overhead cables within reach after gaining access to a roof, what should you do?

A Keep away from them while you work but remember that they are there

B Stop work and confirm that it is safe for you to be on the roof

C Make sure that you are using a wooden ladder

D Hang coloured bunting from them to remind you they are there

**20.33** What should be included in a safety method statement for working at height? Give **three** answers.

A The cost of the job and the time it will take

B The sequence of operations and the equipment to be used

C How much insurance cover will be required

D How falls are to be prevented

E Who will supervise the job on site

**20.34** When it is **not** possible to avoid working above public areas, what should be your **first** consideration?

A To minimise the number of people below at any one time

B To prevent complaints from the public

C To let the public know what you are doing

D To prevent anything falling onto people below

**20.35** Roof light covers should meet which **two** of the following requirements?

A They must be made from the same material as the roof covering

B They must be made from clear material to allow the light through

C They must be strong enough to take the weight of any load placed on them

D They must be waterproof and windproof

E They must be fixed in position to stop them being dislodged

**20.36** Which of these **must** happen before any roof work starts?

A A risk assessment must be carried out following a hierarchy of controls

B The operatives working on the roof must be trained in the use of safety harnesses

C Permits to work must be issued to those allowed to work on the roof

D A weather forecast must be obtained

**20.37** When working at height, what is the **safest** way to transfer waste materials to ground level?

A Through a waste chute directly into a skip

B Asking someone below to keep the area clear of people, then throwing the waste down

C Erecting barriers around the area where the waste will land

D Bagging up the waste before throwing it down

**20.38** If you need to inspect pipework at high level above an asbestos roof, how should you access it?

A Use an extension ladder and crawler board to get to the pipework

B Use a ladder to get onto the roof and walk the bolt line on the roof sheets

C Report the pipework as unsafe

D Hire in suitable mobile access equipment

**20.39** You have been asked to erect specialist access frames using anchor bolts. Before you start work what should you **not** do?

A Check the access frames are sound

B Assume that the access system is safe to use

C Test the anchor bolts

D Ensure that your assistant has their harness on

**20.40** If you are working above a safety net and you notice the net is damaged, what should you do?

A Work somewhere away from the damaged area of net

B Stop work and report it

C Tie the damaged edges together using the net test cords

D See if you can get hold of a harness and lanyard

**20.41** What is the **main** reason for not allowing debris to gather in safety nets?

A It will overload the net

B It looks untidy from below

C It could injure someone who falls into the net

D Small pieces of debris may fall through the net

**20.42** What should you do if you are working at height, but the securing cord for a safety net is in your way?

A Untie the cord, carry out your work and tie it up again

B Untie the cord, but ask the net riggers to re-tie it when you have finished

C Tell the net riggers that you are going to untie the cord

D Leave the cord alone and report the problem

**20.43** Ideally, where should a safety net be rigged?

A Immediately below where you are working

B 2 m below where you are working

C 6 m below where you are working

D At any height below the working position

**20.44** Who should install safety nets?

A A scaffolder

B Someone who has had experience of working with them before

C A trained, competent and authorised person

D A steel or cladding erector

**20.45** When can someone who is **not** a scaffolder remove parts of a scaffold?

A Only if the scaffold is not more than two lifts in height

B As long as a scaffolder refits the parts after the work has finished

C Never, as only competent scaffolders can remove the parts

D Only if they think the parts won't weaken the scaffold

**20.46** What should you do if you find that a scaffold tie is in your way when you are working?

A Ask a scaffolder to remove it

B Remove it yourself and then replace it when you have finished

C Remove it yourself but get a scaffolder to replace it when you have finished

D Report the problem to your supervisor

**20.47** Which type of scaffold tie can be removed by someone who is **not** a scaffolder?

A  A box tie

B  A ring tie

C  A reveal tie

D  No types of tie

# 21 Lifts and escalators

**21.01** Who is allowed to safely release trapped passengers?

A The site manager

B Only a trained and authorised person

C Anyone

D Only the emergency services

**21.02** How should you connect a car light supply to a 240 volt supply (240 volt fused spur)?

A Connect it with the power on

B Switch off the spur and then connect it

C Switch off the spur, remove the fuse and then connect it

D Isolate and lock off the incoming supply and then connect it

**21.03** If a switch needs to be changed in the pit but the isolator is in the machine room 12 floors above, what should you do?

A Isolate the power and then lock and tag the isolator

B Risk assess the situation and change the switch with the power on because it is control voltage

C Use insulated tools

D Stand on a rubber mat

**21.04** What is the main cause of injury and absence for workers in the lift and escalator industry?

A Falls

B Electrocution

C Contact with moving parts

D Manual handling

**21.05** If a counterweight screen is **not** fitted or has been removed, what should you do before starting work?

A Carry out a further risk assessment to establish a safe system of work

B Nothing – just get on with the job as normal

C Give a toolbox talk on guarding

D Issue and wear appropriate personal protective equipment (PPE)

**21.06** Which of the following types of fire extinguisher should **not** be used if there is a fire in a lift or escalator controller?

A Dry chemical

B Water

C Dry powder

D Carbon dioxide

**21.07** What should you do if the lifting accessory you are about to use is defective?

- (A) Only use it for half its safe working load
- (B) Only use it for small lifts under 1 tonne
- (C) Do not use it and inform your supervisor
- (D) Try to fix it

**21.08** If landing doors are **not** fitted to a lift on a construction site, what is the **minimum** height of the barrier that must be fitted instead?

- (A) 650 mm
- (B) 740 mm
- (C) 810 mm
- (D) 950 mm

**21.09** A set of chain blocks has been delivered to site with an examination report stating that they were examined by a competent person a month ago. The hook is obviously damaged. What action do you take?

- (A) Use the blocks as the examination report is current
- (B) Do not use the blocks and inform your supervisor
- (C) Use the blocks at half the safe working load
- (D) Use the blocks until replacement equipment arrives

**21.10** When must you **not** wear rings, bracelets, wrist watches, necklaces and similar items?

- (A) When working near or on electrical or moving equipment
- (B) When working on site generally
- (C) When driving a company vehicle
- (D) After leaving home for work

**21.11** What is the correct method for disposing of used or contaminated oil?

- (A) Decant it into a sealed container and place in a skip
- (B) Dispose of it through a registered waste process
- (C) Dilute it with water and pour it down a sink
- (D) Pour it down a roadside drain

**21.12** A large, heavy, balance weight frame is delivered to site on a lorry with no crane and there is no lifting equipment available on site. What should you do?

- (A) Unload it manually
- (B) Arrange for it to be re-delivered on a suitable lorry
- (C) Slide it down planks
- (D) Tip the load off the lorry

**21.13** A lifting beam at the top of the lift shaft is marked with a safe working load of 800 kg but the brickwork around the beam is cracked and appears to be loose. What should you do?

A Use the beam as normal

B Only lift loads not exceeding 400 kg

C Not use the beam and speak to your supervisor

D De-rate the beam by 75%

**21.14** What is fitted to prevent injury from an overspeed governor?

A A rope

B A restrictor

C A guard

D A switch

**21.15** If the escalator or passenger conveyor has an external machine room, which statement applies to its access doors?

A They should be capable of being locked from both sides and be marked with an appropriate safety sign

B They should be smoke proof in case of a fire

C They should be unlocked at all times in case of an emergency

D They should be capable of being locked on the inside only and be marked with the appropriate safety sign

**21.16** What is the statutory period of examination for lifting equipment that is used to lift people?

A At least monthly

B At least every six months

C At least every 12 months

D Once every two years

**21.17** What checks do you need to carry out before using lifting equipment?

A A drop check

B That it is free from defects and has a current examination certificate

C That the chains are knotted to the correct length

D That the lifting tackle states the date of manufacture

**21.18** Following the initial inspection, how often should a scaffold in a lift shaft be inspected by a competent person?

A At least every day

B At least every seven days

C At least every 14 days

D There is no set period between inspections

**21.19** When installing a new rope, what should you do if you notice a damaged section where something heavy has fallen onto the coil?

A Fit the rope anyway

B Cut out the damaged section

C Reject the rope

D Add an extra termination

**21.20** What must you do **first**, before entering the pit of an operating lift?

A Fit pit props

B Verify the pit stop switch

C Switch the lift off

D Position the access ladder

**21.21** Who should fit a padlock and tag to an electrical lock-out guard?

A Anyone authorised to work on the unit

B Only the person who fitted the lock-out guard

C Only the senior engineer

D Only the manufacturer

**21.22** If you arrive on site and find the lift mains isolator switched off, what should you do?

A Switch it on and get on with your work

B Switch it on and check the safety circuits to see if there is a fault

C Contact the person in control of the premises to find out if they had switched it off

D Shout down the shaft and, if no-one responds, switch it on and get on with your work

**21.23** Which **two** of the following actions must be carried out by an authorised person working alone?

A Registering their presence with the site representative before starting work

B Ensuring their timesheet is accurate and countersigned

C Establishing suitable arrangements to ensure the monitoring of their wellbeing

D Notifying the site manager of the details of their work

E Ensuring that the lift pit is free from water and debris

**21.24** Which statement is **true** when using an authorised lifting accessory marked with its safe working load?

A Never exceed the safe working load

B The safe working load is only for guidance

C Halve the safe working load if the equipment is damaged

D Double the safe working load if people need to be lifted

**21.25** What should be fitted to the main sheave and diverter to prevent injury from rotating equipment?

A Movement sensors

B Guards

C Clutching assemblies

D Safety notices

**21.26** What are the appropriate types of tools and equipment for working on electrical lift-control equipment?

A Insulated tools and an insulating mat

B Non-insulated tools

C Any tools and an insulating mat

D No tools are allowed near electrical equipment

**21.27** When installing a partially enclosed or observation lift, what safe system of work can you use to prevent injury to people below?

A Put up a sign

B Do not use heavy tools

C Secure tools to prevent them falling off

D Only carry out essential work using minimum tools

**21.28** What needs to be checked before any hot work takes place in the lift installation?

A The weight and size of the welding equipment

B How long the task will take

C If a hot-work permit is required

D If the local fire services need to be notified

**21.29** What **must** you ensure if the trapdoor or hatch has to be left open while you work in the machine room?

A That a sign is posted to warn others that you are working there

B That the distance from the trapdoor or hatch to the floor below does not exceed 2 m

C That there is sufficient light available for the work

D That a suitable barrier is put in place around the trapdoor or hatch

**21.30** What **must** you ensure to prevent unauthorised access to unoccupied machine equipment space?

A That the access door is locked

B That a sign is posted to warn trespassers

C That the power supply is isolated

D That a person is posted to prevent access

**21.31** What should be applied to the main isolator of a traction lift to prevent it starting accidentally?

A A warning notice

B A lock-out device

C An RCD (residual current device)

D Lower-rated fuses

**21.32** Who is responsible for the keys when a padlock has been applied to a lock-out device?

A The individual applying the lock

B The site supervisor

C The site manager

D The person nearest the lock-out device

**21.33** If the main contractor wants to use an unfinished lift to move some equipment to an upper floor, what should you do?

A Help to ensure the load is correctly positioned

B Tell them to talk to your supervisor

C Ask for the weight of the equipment

D Allow them to use the lift but take no responsibility for any accidents

**21.34** What is an essential action before gaining access into the escalator or passenger conveyor?

A That the mains switch is locked out and tagged

B That the mains switch is in the on position

C That all steps are removed

D That the drive mechanism is lubricated

**21.35** What is secured at the entry and exit points of an escalator or passenger conveyor to prevent people falling into the machine or machine space?

A Safety barriers

B Safety notices

C Escalator machine equipment guards

D Machine tank covers

**21.36** What **must** you do before moving the steps or pallet band of an escalator or passenger conveyor?

A Check that there are no sharp edges on the steps

B Check that there is a clear route of escape

C Check that no unauthorised people are on the equipment

D Check that a fire extinguisher is available

**21.37** What is the **minimum** size of gap between the edge of the work platform and the hoist way wall that is regarded as a fall hazard?

A 250 mm

B 300 mm

C 330 mm

D 450 mm

**21.38** When is it acceptable to work on the top of a car without a top-of-car control station?

A When the unit has been locked out and tagged

B When two engineers are working on it

C When there is no other way to work on it

D When only one person is working on it

**21.39** Which statement is **true** when working on an energised car?

A Always attach your lanyard to the car top while standing on the landing

B Make sure you step onto the landing with your lanyard still attached to the car

C Always check your lanyard is unclipped before getting off the car top

D Ensure that your lanyard is clipped to a guide bracket or similar anchorage on the shaft

**21.40** What is the **last** thing you should do before getting off a car top through open landing doors when the car-top control is within 1 m of the landing threshold?

A Set the car-top control to test

B Ensure that the car-top stop button is set to stop and the car-top control remains set to test

C Turn off the shaft lights and switch the car-top control to normal

D Press the stop button and switch the car-top control to normal

**21.41** What precaution **must** you take if the landing doors are to be open while work goes on in the lift pit?

A Erect a suitable barrier and secure it in front of the landing doors

B Post a notice on the wall next to the doors

C Do the job when there are not many people about

D Ask someone to guard the open doors while you work

**21.42** What is the **first** thing to do after opening the landing doors and before accessing the car-top of an operating lift?

A Chock the landing doors open

B Press the car-top stop button

C Make sure the lift has stopped

D Put the car-top control in the test position

**21.43** When you gain access to a car top, how should you test that the car-top stop switch operates correctly?

A By trying to move the car in the up direction

B By trying to move the car in the down direction

C By measuring with a multimeter

D By flicking the switch on and off rapidly

**21.44** When working in the pit, when should the lift **not** be positioned towards the top of the shaft?

A When the hydraulic fluid level is low

B When the power supply is cut

C When you are testing the buffers

D When work needs to be done on the underside of the lift

**21.45** What is required on each landing of a new lift shaft before entrances and doors are fitted?

A A warning notice

B A substantial secure barrier to prevent falls

C Orange plastic netting across the opening

D Bright lighting

**21.46** When handling stainless steel car panels, which of the following items of personal protective equipment (PPE) should you wear in addition to safety footwear?

A Suitable safety gloves, such as rigger type gloves

B Hand barrier cream

C Latex gloves

D Hearing protection

**21.47** At what stage in the installation of a lift should guarding be fitted to the lift machine?

A At the end of the job

B During commissioning

C When handing over to the client

D Before the machine can be operated

**21.48** Which of these statements is **not** true?

A A stop switch must be within 1.5 m of the front of the car

B The car top should be clean and free from grease and oil spills

C You should secure your tools out of your standing area when working on top of the car

D Before trying to access the hoist way, you should decide whether the work will need the power supply to be live

**21.49** What is the **most** effective way of reducing the likelihood of being struck by falling objects?

A Don't work below another person

B Wear a safety helmet with a chin strap

C Put warning signs up in the area

D Install suitable debris netting

# 22 Tunnelling

**22.01** When working underground how quickly should you be able to get to your self-rescue set?

A It must be within one minute's walking distance

B It must be immediately available

C It must be within three minutes' walking distance

D It must be within two minutes' walking distance

**22.02** In the event of an emergency who will use the information displayed on a tally board?

A The Health and Safety Executive (HSE)

B The crane operator

C The rescue services

D Environmental Health

**22.03** If oxygen levels are dropping, at what point would the atmosphere be classed as oxygen deficient?

A 18%

B 19%

C 20%

D 21%

**22.04** Methane gas does **not** have an odour. In what **two** ways can it be dangerous?

A It causes skin irritation

B It can cause temporary blindness

C It is explosive

D It is toxic

E It reduces oxygen in the atmosphere

**22.05** Which of the following is a reliable way to detect carbon monoxide and methane gas?

A They both have a distinctive bad egg smell

B With a dosimeter

C With a calibrated gas detector

D With your eyes, as you can see the gases in the mist

**22.06** How could hydrogen sulphide affect those working in a tunnel?

A It can leave a yellow dust which can irritate the skin

B It can make it noisier and therefore harder for you to hear

C It can cause a mist making it difficult to see

D It can cause respiratory paralysis, stopping you from breathing

F 22

**22.07** How would you know if the ventilation system stops working?

A You would be told at the daily start of shift briefing

B You would be informed as part of your induction

C An audible alarm would sound

D Your supervisor would inform you

**22.08** Nitrogen oxide (NO) gas can be present in tunnels. Which of these plant items causes the **most** nitrogen oxide to be generated or made?

A Tunnel-boring machines (TBMs)

B Electro-hydraulic spray pumps

C Rail-mounted plant

D Diesel-powered equipment

**22.09** Exposure to nitrogen oxide (NO) gas can cause breathing problems. Which of the following should be the **first** control measure?

A Provide air monitoring

B Have a portable breathing set nearby

C Avoid exposure

D Provide ventilation systems

**22.10** How should communication equipment be powered?

A Linked to the main tunnel power supply

B Independent of the main tunnel power supply

C Linked to the 33 kVA power supply

D Battery-powered

**22.11** Which **two** methods are commonly used for communication between the tunnelling face and the surface?

A Email

B Two-way radio

C Telephone

D Text message

E Tannoy system

**22.12** What is the **maximum** recommended distance between emergency lighting in a tunnel?

A 25 m

B 50 m

C 75 m

D 100 m

**22.13** What is the colour of a 400 volt plug?

(A) Black

(B) Blue

(C) Yellow

(D) Red

**22.14** When charging lead acid batteries they produce an explosive gas. Smoking and other naked flames are **not** permitted within what distance of a battery-charging area?

(A) 5 m

(B) 10 m

(C) 15 m

(D) 20 m

**22.15** Hot work activities are **not** permitted within what distance of a diesel-fuelling point?

(A) 5 m

(B) 10 m

(C) 15 m

(D) 20 m

**22.16** As a **minimum**, how long **must** a fire watch be maintained after hot works have been completed?

(A) 15 minutes

(B) 30 minutes

(C) 45 minutes

(D) 60 minutes

**22.17** What does the term **DCI** refer to in compressed air tunnelling?

(A) Dizzy, confused, induced state

(B) Decompression incident

(C) Decompression, combustion incident

(D) Decompression illness

**22.18** Which of the following characteristics are associated with hydrogen sulphide gas?

(A) A smell of rotten eggs

(B) It causes skin irritation

(C) It is odourless

(D) It causes a yellow haze

**22.19** Which of the following statements is correct regarding hand-arm vibration syndrome?

A It can be prevented if gloves are worn

B It can be partially cured with medication

C It can be corrected by surgery

D It causes irreversible damage

**22.20** What **must** be available at batching plants to deal with cement or concrete splashes?

A A supply of running water

B Sterile bandages

C A first aider

D An eyewash station

**22.21** Which one of the following is **not** a health risk associated with sprayed concrete linings?

A Cement burns

B Arc eye

C Hand-arm vibration syndrome

D Inhalation of dust

**22.22** Which of the following is **not** a hazard associated with hand mining?

A Vibrating hand tools

B Noise

C Falling mined material

D Sprayed concrete rebound

**22.23** When should a hop up or refuge in the tunnel be used?

A When vehicles are passing

B For services such as cables

C When installing ventilation cassettes

D For storage of materials and equipment

**22.24** Which of the following **must** be fitted as a conveyor system safety device?

A Emergency lighting

B Emergency pull cord or stop button

C Hazard lighting

D Seat belt

**22.25** If a locomotive or vehicle is approaching you in the tunnel, when should you make your way to a hop up or safe refuge?

A Immediately

B Only when you can see it

C When you have identified the direction of travel

D Only when everyone else starts to move

**22.26** A locomotive is entering the rear of the tunnel-boring machine. Which **two** electronic systems are recommended to assist in controlling its movements?

A Signal or traffic lights

B CCTV in the cab

C Siren

D Telephone

E Klaxon bell

**22.27** Inclined conveyors are fitted with anti-rollback devices to prevent the belt running backwards due to which **two** potential failures?

A Overloading

B Power loss

C Oil spillage

D Overheating

E Water leak

**22.28** Which of the following is a common traffic light system used underground to control plant movement?

A Red = stop, Amber = out bye, Green = in bye

B Red = stop, Amber = in bye, Green = out bye

C Red = in bye, Amber = stop, Green = out bye

D Red = out bye, Amber = in bye, Green = stop

**22.29** What is the likely hazard from moving plant or locomotives in a tunnel?

A Crush

B Crash

C Noise

D Asphyxiation

**22.30** Which one of the following is the **least** effective method of controlling locomotive movements in the pit bottom?

A Traffic lights

B Radio

C Shouting

D Hand signals

F
22

**22.31** How often should safe-refuge (hop ups) be located along a tunnel?

A 50 m on straights; 25 m on curves

B 60 m on straights; 30 m on curves

C 70 m on straights; 25 m on curves

D 80 m on straights; 20 m on curves

**22.32** The tunnel-boring machine operator has restricted vision during the building process. Which of the following is the **most** effective way of overcoming this?

A Alternative control point

B Mirrors at shoulder or crane level

C Use a signaller

D Get one of the gang to build

**22.33** What is the **first** action to be taken if there is a blockage in the grouting pipe?

A Locate the blockage

B Split the line

C Clean out section by section

D Release the pressure in the pipeline

**22.34** Why is it important to clean grouting pipelines after use?

A It helps prevent blockages, which could cause the hose to burst

B It helps prevent the pipes from becoming weakened

C It keeps the dust level below the point that respiratory protective equipment (RPE) is needed

D It prevents the atmosphere from becoming explosive

**22.35** Crash cages and side bars or sliding doors should be fitted to all personnel carrying cars used in the tunnel. Select **two** reasons why they are needed.

A To prevent derailment of the personnel carrying car

B To minimise injury in the event of a derailment

C To allow personnel to talk while being transported

D To stop personnel sitting close together

E To prevent personnel leaning out or falling out

**22.36** For tunnelling operations what is the **minimum** number of escape routes or methods that **must** be maintained from a working shaft?

A One

B Two

C Three

D Four

F
22

**22.37** What term is used for the access and egress control system to tunnels?

A Visitor book

B Tally system

C Signing-in book

D Clocking on machine

**22.38** If a personnel carrying cage is used to transport workers into and out of a shaft, how many people can be transported at any one time?

A As defined by the Health and Safety Executive (HSE)

B As many as can fit into it

C As many as is stated on the personnel carrier

D As many as is stated by the supervisor

**22.39** What is the **minimum** recommended height of a secure barrier used to prevent falls around an open shaft?

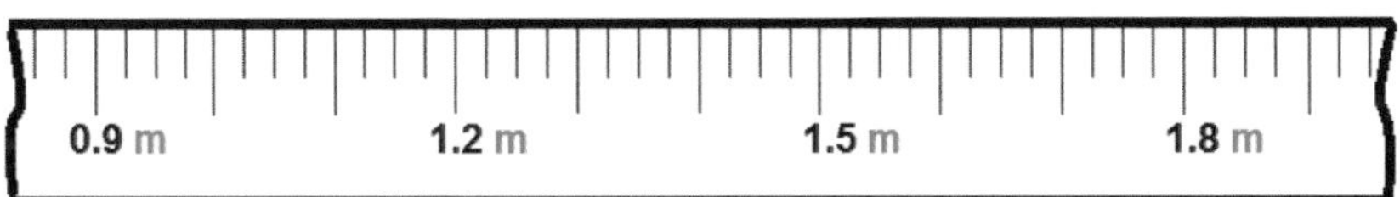


**22.40** Which of the following situations would require using a safety harness?

A Working as the signaller at the pit top

B Working as the belt-person on a TBM

C Landing concrete jacking-pipes in the pit bottom

D Building rings from a platform within a shaft

**22.41** Oxygen cylinders should **not** be allowed to come into contact with which of the following substances?

A Mud

B Grease

C Paint

D Air

**22.42** While walking through the tunnel you see a tear in the ventilation ducting. What should you do?

(A) Report it to your supervisor

(B) Try to repair it

(C) Check if it has got any bigger at the end of the shift

(D) Evacuate the tunnel

**22.43** A grout gun inserted into a segment grout hole may present which of the following hazards?

(A) Shrinking grout hose

(B) Falls from height

(C) Blowout at injection point

(D) Hand-arm vibration

**22.44** Which of the following personal protective equipment (PPE) is **not** normally required for robotic-sprayed concrete lining operations in tunnelling?

(A) Eye protection

(B) Respiratory protective equipment

(C) Disposable overalls

(D) Safety harness

# 23 HVACR – Heating and plumbing services

**23.01** If you have to drill through a wall panel that you suspect contains an asbestos material, what should you do?

A Use a low speed drill setting

B Spray it with water as you drill

C Put on a dust mask before you drill

D Stop work and report it

**23.02** When a new piece of plant has been installed but has **not** been commissioned, how should it be left?

A With all valves and switches turned off

B With all valves and switches clearly labelled

C With all valves and switches locked off

D With all valves and switches turned on and ready to use

**23.03** Who can solder a fitting on an isolated copper gas pipe?

A A plumber

B A pipefitter

C A skilled welder

D A Gas Safe registered engineer

**23.04** When working in a riser, how should access be controlled?

A By a site security operative

B By those who are working in it

C By the main contractor

D By a permit to work system

**23.05** If you find a coloured wire sticking out of an electrical plug what is the correct action to take?

A Push it back into the plug and carry on working

B Pull the wire clear of the plug and report it to your supervisor

C Mark the item as defective and follow your company procedure for defective items

D Take the plug apart and carry out a repair

**23.06** How should extension leads in use on site be positioned?

A They should be located so as to prevent a tripping hazard

B They should be laid out in the shortest, most convenient route

C They should be coiled on a drum or cable tidy

D They should be raised on bricks

**23.07** What should you do if you need additional temporary wiring for your power tools whilst working on site?

A. Find some cable and extend the wiring yourself

B. Stop work until an authorised supply has been installed

C. Speak to an electrician and ask them to do the temporary wiring

D. Disconnect a longer cable serving somewhere else and reconnect it to where you need it

**23.08** Which item of electrical equipment does **not** require portable appliance testing?

A. Battery-powered rechargeable drill

B. 110 volt electrical drill

C. 110 volt portable halogen light

D. Electric kettle

**23.09** Why is temporary continuity bonding carried out before removing and replacing sections of metallic pipework?

A. To provide a continuous earth for the pipework installation

B. To prevent any chance of blowing a fuse

C. To maintain the live supply to the electrical circuit

D. To prevent any chance of corrosion to the pipework

**23.10** Which type of power drill is **most** suitable for fixing a run of pipework outside in wet weather?

A. Battery-powered drill

B. Drill with 110 volt power supply

C. Drill with 240 volt power supply

D. Any mains voltage drill with a power breaker

**23.11** What would you use to find out whether a wall into which you are about to drill contains an electric supply?

A. A neon screwdriver

B. A cable tracer

C. A multimeter

D. A hammer and chisel

**23.12** Where should liquefied petroleum gas (LPG) cylinders be positioned when supplying an appliance in a site cabin?

A. Inside the cabin in a locked cupboard

B. Under the cabin

C. Inside the cabin next to the appliance

D. Outside the cabin

**23.13** How should you position the exhaust of an engine-driven generator that has to be run inside a building?

A Outside the building

B In a stairwell

C In another room

D In a riser

**23.14** How should cylinders containing liquefied petroleum gas (LPG) be stored on site?

A In a locked cellar with clear warning signs

B In a locked cage at least 3 m from any oxygen cylinders

C Within a secure storage container at the back of the site

D Covered by a tarpaulin to shield the compressed cylinder from sunlight

**23.15** If you spill some oil on the floor and you do **not** have any absorbent material to clean the area, what should you do?

A Spread it about to lessen the depth

B Keep people out of the area and inform your supervisor

C Do nothing, as it will eventually soak into the floor

D Warn other people as they tread through it

**23.16** If you find a dangerous gas fitting that is likely to cause a death or specified injury, who **must** be sent a formal report?

A The client

B The gas board

C The health and safety manager

D The Health and Safety Executive (HSE)

**23.17** When **must** you wear eye protection while drilling through a wall?

A Only when drilling overhead

B Only when the drill bit exceeds 20 mm

C Always, whatever the circumstances

D Only when drilling through concrete

**23.18** What personal protective equipment (PPE) should you wear when using a hammer drill to drill a 100 mm diameter hole through a brick wall?

A Gloves, breathing apparatus and boots

B Ear defenders, respiratory protective equipment, boots and eye protection

C Ear defenders, breathing apparatus and barrier cream

D Barrier cream, boots and respiratory protective equipment

**23.19** What should you do when using pipe-freezing equipment to isolate a damaged section of pipe?

(A) Always work in pairs when using pipe-freezing equipment

(B) Never allow the freezing gas to come into direct contact with surface water

(C) Never use pipe-freezing equipment on plastic pipe

(D) Wear gloves to avoid direct contact with the skin and read the COSHH assessment

**23.20** If you are working where welding is being carried out, what should be provided to protect you from welding flash?

(A) A fire extinguisher

(B) Warning notices

(C) Screens

(D) A hi-vis vest

**23.21** When using a blowtorch to joint copper tube and fittings in a domestic property, how should a fire extinguisher be made available?

(A) It should be available in the immediate work area

(B) It should be held over the joint while you are using the blowtorch

(C) It should be kept away from the work area in case a spark causes it to explode

(D) It should be available only if a property is occupied

**23.22** If you are carrying out hot works with a blowtorch, when should you stop using it?

(A) Just before you leave the site

(B) At least one hour before you leave the site

(C) At least two hours before you leave the site

(D) At least four hours before you leave the site

**23.23** What should you do when using a blowtorch near to flexible pipe lagging?

(A) Remove the lagging at least 1 m either side of the work

(B) Remove just enough lagging to carry out the work

(C) Remove the lagging at least 3 m either side of the work

(D) Wet the lagging but leave it in place

**23.24** What should you do when using a blowtorch near to timber?

(A) Carry out the work, taking care not to set fire to the timber

(B) Wet the timber first and have a bucket of water handy

(C) Use a non-combustible mat and have a fire extinguisher in the immediate work area

(D) Point the flame away from the timber and have a bucket of sand ready to put out the fire

**23.25** The legionella bacteria that cause legionnaires' disease are **most** likely to be found in which of the following?

A. A boiler operating at a temperature of 80°C

B. An infrequently used shower hose outlet

C. A cold water storage cistern containing water at 10°C

D. A toilet pan

**23.26** How are legionella bacteria passed on to humans?

A. Through fine water droplets, such as sprays or mists

B. By drinking dirty water

C. Through contact with the skin

D. From other people when they sneeze

**23.27** When planning a lifting operation, how should the sequence of operations to enable a safe lift be confirmed?

A. Using verbal instruction

B. In a method statement

C. In a radio telephone message

D. On a notice in the canteen

**23.28** Which of these is **true** in relation to the safe working load (SWL) of lifting equipment?

A. It is never marked on the equipment but kept with the test certificates

B. It is provided for guidance only

C. It may be exceeded by no more than 25%

D. It is the maximum safe working load

**23.29** What **must** be clearly marked on all lifting equipment?

A. The name of the manufacturer

B. The safe working load

C. The next test date

D. The specification of material from which it is made

**23.30** What is the **safest** method of transporting long lengths of copper pipe by van?

A. Tying the pipes to the roof with copper wire

B. Someone holding the pipes on the roof rack as you drive along

C. Putting the pipes inside the van with the ends out of the passenger window

D. Using a pipe rack fixed to the roof of the van

**23.31** What is the **safest** way to move a cast iron boiler some distance?

A Get a workmate to carry it with you

B Drag it

C Roll it end-over-end

D Use a trolley or other manual handling aid

**23.32** During a job you may need to work below a ground-level suspended timber floor. What is the **most** important question you should ask?

A Can the work be performed from outside?

B Will temporary lighting be used?

C How many days will the work take to complete?

D Could Weil's disease (leptospirosis) be a problem?

**23.33** When carrying a ladder on a vehicle, what is the correct way of securing the ladder to the roof rack?

A Rope

B Bungee elastics

C Ladder clamps

D Copper wire

**23.34** What **must** you ensure before using a ladder?

A That it is secured to prevent it from moving sideways or sliding outwards

B That no-one else has booked the ladder for their work

C That an apprentice or workmate is standing by in case you slip and fall

D That the weather forecast is for a bright, clear day

**23.35** When positioning and erecting a stepladder, which of the following is essential for its safe use?

A It has a tool tray towards the top of the steps

B The restraint mechanism is spread to its full extent

C You will be able to reach the job by standing on the top step

D Your supervisor has positioned and erected the steps

**23.36** What is the recommended **maximum** height for a free-standing mobile tower?

A There is no recommended height

B 2 m

C The height recommended by the manufacturer

D 12 m

**23.37** What is the **first** thing you should do after getting on to the platform of a correctly erected mobile tower?

A Check that the brakes are locked on

B Check for overhead power lines

C Check that the access hatch has been closed to prevent falls of personnel, tools or equipment

D Check that the tower does not rock or wobble

**23.38** What should be done before a mobile tower is moved?

A All people and equipment must be removed from the platform

B A permit to work must be issued

C The principal contractor must give their approval

D Arrangements must be made with the forklift truck driver

**23.39** What must be done **first** before any roof work is carried out?

A A risk assessment must be carried out

B The operatives working on the roof must be trained in the use of safety harnesses

C Permits to work must be issued only to those allowed to work on the roof

D A weather forecast must be obtained

**23.40** What is edge protection designed to do?

A Make access to the roof easier

B Secure tools and materials close to the edge

C Prevent rainwater running off the roof onto workers below

D Prevent the fall of people and materials

**23.41** When assembling a mobile tower what major hazard **must** you be aware of?

A Water pipes

B Cable trays

C False ceilings

D Overhead service cables

**23.42** What should folding stepladders be used for?

A General access on site

B Short-term work

C All site activities where a straight ladder cannot be used

D Getting on and off mobile towers

**23.43** When drilling a hole for a boiler flue outside, which type of working platform should you use?

A A long ladder

B Borrowed scaffolding that you have erected

C A mobile tower or fixed scaffold

D Packing cases to stand on

**23.44** How should you access a roof to install a flexible flue liner into an existing chimney?

A Work from a roof ladder securely hooked over the ridge

B Use an access scaffold designed for chimney works

C Scramble up the roof tiles to get to the chimney

D Get your mate to do the job while you hold a rope tied to them

**23.45** What is the **only** circumstance where stepladders should be used?

A Inside buildings

B If no other suitable equipment is available after works have been risk assessed

C If they are made of aluminium

D If they are less than 1.75 m high

# 24 HVACR – Pipefitting and welding

**24.01** When a new piece of plant has been installed but has **not** been commissioned, how should it be left?

A With all valves and switches turned off

B With all valves and switches clearly labelled

C With all valves and switches locked off

D With all valves and switches turned on and ready to use

**24.02** Who is allowed to install natural gas pipework?

A A skilled engineer

B A pipefitter

C A Gas Safe registered engineer

D Anybody

**24.03** Who should carry out pressure testing on pipework or vessels?

A Anyone who is available

B A competent person

C A Health and Safety Executive (HSE) inspector

D A building control officer

**24.04** When working in a riser, how should access be controlled?

A By a site security operative

B By those who are working in it

C By the main contractor

D By a permit to work system

**24.05** While working on your own and tracing pipework in a building, you notice that the pipes enter a service duct. What should you do?

A Go into the service duct and continue to trace the pipework

B Ask someone in the building to act as your second person

C Put on your personal protective equipment (PPE) and carry on with the job

D Stop work until a risk assessment has been carried out

**24.06** If you find a coloured wire sticking out of an electrical plug what is the correct action to take?

A Push it back into the plug and carry on working

B Pull the wire clear of the plug and report it to your supervisor

C Mark the item as defective and follow your company procedure for defective items

D Take the plug apart and carry out a repair

**24.07** How should extension leads in use on site be positioned?

- A They should be located so as to prevent a tripping hazard
- B They should be laid out in the shortest, most convenient route
- C They should be coiled on a drum or cable tidy
- D They should be raised on bricks

**24.08** What should you do if you need additional temporary wiring for your power tools whilst working on site?

- A Find some cable and extend the wiring yourself
- B Stop work until an authorised supply has been installed
- C Speak to an electrician and ask them to do the temporary wiring
- D Disconnect a longer cable serving somewhere else and reconnect it to where you need it

**24.09** Which item of electrical equipment does **not** require portable appliance testing?

- A Battery-powered rechargeable drill
- B 110 volt electrical drill
- C 110 volt portable halogen light
- D Electric kettle

**24.10** Where should liquefied petroleum gas (LPG) cylinders be positioned when supplying an appliance in a site cabin?

- A Inside the cabin in a locked cupboard
- B Under the cabin
- C Inside the cabin next to the appliance
- D Outside the cabin

**24.11** How should you position the exhaust of an engine-driven generator that has to be run inside a building?

- A Outside the building
- B In a stairwell
- C In another room
- D In a riser

**24.12** How should cylinders containing liquefied petroleum gas (LPG) be stored on site?

- A In a locked cellar with clear warning signs
- B In a locked cage at least 3 m from any oxygen cylinders
- C As close to the point of use as possible
- D Covered by a tarpaulin to shield the compressed cylinder from sunlight

**24.13** If you spill some oil on the floor and you do **not** have any absorbent material to clean the area, what should you do?

A Spread it about to lessen the depth

B Keep people out of the area and inform your supervisor

C Do nothing, as it will eventually soak into the floor

D Warn other people as they tread through it

**24.14** What guarding is required when a pipe threading machine is in use?

A A length of red material hung from the exposed end of the pipe

B A barrier at the exposed end of the pipe only

C A barrier around the whole of the pipe length and machine

D Warning notices in the work area

**24.15** What should you do when using pipe-freezing equipment to isolate a damaged section of pipe?

A Always work in pairs

B Never allow the freezing gas to come into direct contact with surface water

C Never use pipe-freezing equipment on plastic pipe

D Wear gloves to avoid direct contact with your skin and read the COSHH assessment

**24.16** Why is it important to know the difference between propane and butane equipment?

A Propane equipment operates at higher pressure

B Propane equipment operates at lower pressure

C Propane equipment is cheaper

D Propane equipment can be used with smaller, easy-to-handle cylinders

**24.17** Which of the following statements is **true**?

A Both propane and butane are heavier than air

B Butane is heavier than air while propane is lighter than air

C Propane is heavier than air while butane is lighter than air

D Both propane and butane are lighter than air

**24.18** Apart from the cylinders used in gas-powered forklift trucks, why should liquefied petroleum gas (LPG) cylinders **never** be placed on their side during use?

A It would give a faulty reading on the contents gauge, resulting in flashback

B Air could be drawn into the cylinder, creating a dangerous mixture of gases

C The liquid gas would be at too low a level to allow the torch to burn correctly

D The liquid gas could be drawn from the cylinder, creating a safety hazard

**24.19** What is the method of checking for leaks after connecting a liquefied petroleum gas (LPG) regulator to the bottle?

A Test with a lighted match

B Sniff the connections to detect the smell of gas

C Listen to hear for escaping gas

D Apply leak detection fluid to the connections

**24.20** What is the **most** likely risk of injury when cutting a pipe with hand-operated pipe cutters?

A Your fingers may become trapped between the cutting wheel and the pipe

B You may cut yourself on the inside edge of the cut pipe

C You may damage your muscles due to continued use

D A piece of sharp metal could fly off and hit you

**24.21** Why is it essential to take great care when handling oxygen cylinders?

A They contain highly flammable compressed gas

B They contain highly flammable liquid gas

C They are filled to extremely high pressures

D They contain poisonous gas

**24.22** When do you need to wear eye protection while drilling through a wall?

A Only when drilling overhead

B Only when the drill bit exceeds 20 mm

C Always, whatever the circumstances

D Only when drilling through concrete

**24.23** If you are working where welding is being carried out, what should be provided to protect you from welding flash?

A A fire extinguisher

B Warning notices

C Screens

D A hi-vis vest

**24.24** What is the main hazard associated with flame-cutting and welding?

A Gas poisoning

B Fire

C Dropping a gas cylinder

D Not having a hot-work permit

**24.25** When should you stop carrying out hot works?

A Just before you leave the site

B At least one hour before you leave the site

C At least two hours before you leave the site

D At least four hours before you leave the site

**24.26** What should you do when using a blowtorch near to flexible pipe lagging?

A Remove the lagging at least 1 m either side of the work

B Remove just enough lagging to carry out the work

C Remove the lagging at least 3 m either side of the work

D Wet the lagging but leave it in place

**24.27** When using a blowtorch near to timber, what should you do?

A Carry out the work taking care not to catch the timber

B Point the flame away from the timber and have a bucket of sand ready to put out the fire

C Wet the timber first and keep a bucket of water handy

D Use a non-combustible mat and have a fire extinguisher ready

**24.28** What is the colour of an acetylene cylinder?

A Orange

B Black

C Green

D Maroon

**24.29** Which item of personal protective equipment (PPE) is designed to protect against infrared radiation damage to the eyes during flame cutting or welding?

A Respiratory protective equipment

B Clear goggles

C Eye protection with a tinted filter lens

D Dust mask

**24.30** When using oxyacetylene brazing equipment, how should the bottles be positioned?

A Laid on their side and secured

B Stood upright and secured

C Stood upside down

D Angled at 45°

**24.31** The use of oxyacetylene equipment is **not** recommended for which jointing method?

A. Jointing copper pipe using hard soldering

B. Jointing copper tube using capillary soldered fittings

C. Jointing mild steel tube

D. Jointing sheet lead

**24.34** Where should acetylene gas-welding bottles be stored when they are **not** in use?

A. Outside in a special storage compound

B. In a special rack in a company van

C. Inside a building in a locked cupboard

D. With oxygen bottles

**24.32** Which **two** of these activities are likely to need a hot-work permit?

Drag your answers into the boxes below

A. Cutting steel with an angle grinder

B. Using the heaters in the drying room

C. Refuelling a diesel dump truck

D. Replacing an empty liquefied petroleum gas (LPG) cylinder with a full one

E. Soldering pipework in a central heating system

**24.33** When planning a lifting operation, how should the sequence of operations to enable a safe lift be confirmed?

A. Using verbal instruction

B. In a method statement

C. In a radio telephone message

D. On a notice in the canteen

**24.35** Which of these statements is **true** in relation to the SWL of lifting equipment?

A. It is never marked on the equipment but kept with the test certificates

B. It is provided for guidance only

C. It may be exceeded by no more than 25%

D. It is the absolute maximum safe working load

**24.36** What **must** be clearly marked on all lifting equipment?

- A The name of the manufacturer
- B The safe working load
- C The next test date
- D The specification of material from which it is made

**24.37** Which **two** of the following are essential safety checks to be carried out before using oxyacetylene equipment?

- A That the cylinders are full
- B That the cylinders, hoses and flashback arresters are in good condition
- C That the trolley wheels are the right size
- D That the area is well ventilated and clear of any obstructions
- E That the cylinders are the right weight

**24.38** Who should be present during the pressure testing of pipework or vessels?

- A The architect
- B The site foreman
- C Only those involved in carrying out the test
- D Anybody

**24.39** What should you ensure when using an electrically powered threading machine?

- A That the power supply is 24 volts
- B That the power supply is 400 volts and the machine is fitted with a guard
- C That your clothing cannot get caught on rotating parts of the machine
- D That the machine is only used in your compound

**24.40** What **must** you ensure before using a ladder?

- A That it is secured to prevent it from moving sideways or sliding outwards
- B That no-one else has booked the ladder for their work
- C That an apprentice or workmate is standing by in case you slip and fall
- D That the weather forecast is for a bright, clear day

**24.41** When positioning and erecting a stepladder, which of the following is essential for its safe use?

- A It has a tool tray towards the top of the steps
- B The restraint mechanism is spread to its full extent
- C You will be able to reach the job by standing on the top step
- D Your supervisor has positioned and erected the steps

F 24

**24.42** What is the recommended **maximum** height for a free-standing mobile tower?

A There is no restriction

B 2 m

C The height recommended by the manufacturer

D 12 m

**24.43** What should be done before a mobile tower is moved?

A All people and equipment must be removed from the platform

B A permit to work must be issued

C The principal contractor must give their approval

D Arrangements must be made with the forklift truck driver

**24.44** What must be done **first** before any roof work is carried out?

A A risk assessment must be carried out

B The operatives working on the roof must be trained in the use of safety harnesses

C Permits to work must be issued only to those allowed to work on the roof

D A weather forecast must be obtained

**24.45** What is edge protection designed to do?

A Make access to the roof easier

B Secure tools and materials close to the edge

C Prevent rainwater running off the roof onto workers below

D Prevent the fall of people and materials

**24.46** What is the **first** thing you should do after getting on to the platform of a correctly erected mobile tower?

A Check that the brakes are locked on

B Check for overhead power lines

C Close the access hatch to prevent falls of personnel, tools or equipment

D Make sure that the tower does not rock or wobble

**24.47** When assembling a mobile tower what major hazard **must** you be aware of?

A Water pipes

B Cable trays

C False ceilings

D Overhead service cables

**24.48** If you are asked to install high-level ductwork from a platform that has no edge protection and is located above an open stairwell, what should you do?

A) Get on with the job, but keep away from the edge of the platform

B) Not start work until your work platform has been fitted with guard-rails and toe-boards

C) Get on with the job, ensuring that a workmate stays close by

D) Get on with the job, provided that if you fall the stairwell guard-rail will prevent you from falling further

# 25 HVACR – Ductwork

**25.01** When a new piece of plant has been installed but has **not** been commissioned, how should it be left?

A With all valves and switches turned off

B With all valves and switches clearly labelled

C With all valves and switches locked off

D With all valves and switches turned on and ready to use

**25.02** Who should carry out leakage testing of a newly installed ductwork system?

A The installation contractor

B The property owner

C The designer

D A trained and competent person

**25.03** When working in a riser, how should access be controlled?

A By a site security operative

B By those who are working in it

C By the main contractor

D By a permit to work system

**25.04** If you find a coloured wire sticking out of an electrical plug what is the correct action to take?

A Push it back into the plug and carry on working

B Pull the wire clear of the plug and report it to your supervisor

C Mark the item as defective and follow your company procedure for defective items

D Take the plug apart and carry out a repair

**25.05** How should extension leads in use on site be positioned?

A They should be located so as to prevent a tripping hazard

B They should be laid out in the shortest, most convenient route

C They should be coiled on a drum or cable tidy

D They should be raised on bricks

**25.06** What should you do if you need additional temporary wiring for your power tools whilst working on site?

A Find some cable and extend the wiring yourself

B Stop work until an authorised supply has been installed

C Speak to an electrician and ask them to do the temporary wiring

D Disconnect a longer cable serving somewhere else and reconnect it to where you need it

**25.07** Which item of electrical equipment does **not** require portable appliance testing?

A Battery-powered rechargeable drill

B 110 volt electrical drill

C 110 volt portable halogen light

D Electric kettle

**25.08** Where should liquefied petroleum gas (LPG) cylinders be positioned when supplying an appliance in a site cabin?

A Inside the cabin in a locked cupboard

B Under the cabin

C Inside the cabin next to the appliance

D Outside the cabin

**25.09** How should you position the exhaust of an engine-driven generator that has to be run inside a building?

A Outside the building

B In a stairwell

C In another room

D In a riser

**25.10** If you spill some oil on the floor and you do **not** have any absorbent material to clean the area, what should you do?

A Spread it about to lessen the depth

B Keep people out of the area and inform your supervisor

C Do nothing, as it will eventually soak into the floor

D Warn other people as they tread through it

**25.11** Which **two** of the following should you use when cutting aluminium or tin ductwork that has been pre-insulated with fibreglass?

A A hacksaw

B Respiratory protective equipment

C A chisel

D A set of tin snips

E A blowtorch

**25.12** A person who has been using a solvent-based ductwork sealant is complaining of headaches and feeling sick. What is the **first** thing you should do?

A Let them carry on working but try to keep a close watch on them

B Get them a drink of water and a headache tablet

C Get them out to fresh air and make them rest

D Make an entry in the accident book

**25.13** What additional control measure **must** be put in place when welding in-situ galvanised ductwork?

A Screens

B Fume extraction

C Warning signs

D Hearing protection

**25.14** When jointing plastic-coated metal ductwork, which of the following methods of jointing presents the **most** serious risk to health?

A Welding

B Taping

C Riveting

D Fixing nuts and bolts

**25.15** If you are removing a run of ductwork in an unoccupied building and notice a hypodermic syringe behind it, what should you do?

A Ensure the syringe is empty, remove it and place it with the rubbish

B Wear gloves, break the syringe into small pieces and flush it down the drain

C Notify the supervisor, cordon off the area and call the emergency services

D Wear gloves, use grips to remove the syringe to a safe place and report your find

**25.16** If you are working where welding is being carried out, what should be provided to protect you from welding flash?

A A fire extinguisher

B Warning notices

C Screens

D A hi-vis vest

**25.17** When planning a lifting operation, how should the sequence of operations to enable a safe lift be confirmed?

A By verbal instructions

B In a method statement

C In a radio telephone message

D Via a notice in the canteen

**25.18** Which of these statements is **true** in relation to the SWL of lifting equipment?

A It is never marked on the equipment but kept with the test certificates

B It is provided for guidance only

C It may be exceeded by no more than 25%

D It is the absolute maximum safe working load

**25.19** What **must** be clearly marked on all lifting equipment?

A The name of the manufacturer

B The safe working load

C The next test date

D The specification of material from which it is made

**25.20** When using a material hoist you notice that the lifting cable is frayed. What should you do?

A Get the job done as quickly as possible

B Straighten out the cable using mole grips

C Do not use the hoist, and report the problem

D Be very careful when using the hoist

**25.21** When do you need to wear eye protection while drilling through a wall?

A Only when drilling overhead

B Only when the drill bit exceeds 20 mm

C Always, whatever the circumstances

D Only when drilling through concrete

**25.22** In addition to a safety helmet and protective footwear, what personal protective equipment (PPE) should you wear when using a hammer drill?

A Gloves and breathing apparatus

B Hearing protection, respiratory protective equipment and eye protection

C Hearing protection, breathing apparatus and barrier cream

D Barrier cream and respiratory protective equipment

**25.23** How should you leave the area around ductwork after using a solvent-based sealant?

A Seal up all the open ends to ensure that dirt cannot get into the system

B Ensure that the lids are left off tins of solvent

C Remove any safety signs or notices

D Leave inspection covers off and erect no smoking signs

**25.24** Before taking down a run of ductwork, what is the **first** thing you should do?

A Assess the volume of waste and get an appropriate sized skip

B Cut through the support rods

C Clean the ductwork to remove all dust

D Assess the task to be undertaken and check its support system

**25.25** What is the **safest** way to move a fan-coil unit some distance?

A Get a workmate to carry it with you

B Drag it

C Roll it end-over-end

D Use a trolley or other manual handling aid

**25.26** While fitting a fire damper into a ductwork system you notice that, due to a manufacturing fault, it may **not** operate properly. What should you do?

A Install it anyway, as it is

B Fix it so that it stays open, and then install it

C Not fit the damper and report the fault

D Leave it out of the ductwork system altogether

**25.27** If you have to dismantle some waste-extract ductwork, what is the **first** thing you should do?

A Arrange for a skip to put it in

B Ensure there is a certificate of cleanliness in place before commencing work

C Check that the duct supports are strong enough to cope with the dismantling

D Make sure there are enough disc cutters to do the job

**25.28** If you are using a genie hoist and notice that part of the hoist is buckling slightly, what should you do?

A Lower the load immediately

B Carry on with the job, while keeping an eye on the buckling metal

C Straighten out the buckled metal and then get on with the lifting operation

D Get the job finished quickly

**25.29** When carrying out solvent welding on plastic ductwork, what particular safety measure **must** be applied?

A The area must be well ventilated

B The supervisor must be present

C A hard hat must be worn

D It must be done in daylight

**25.30** Which of the following do you **not** need to do before using a cleaning agent or biocide in a ductwork system?

A Ask for advice from the cleaning agent or biocide manufacturer

B Read the COSHH assessment for the material, carry out a risk assessment and produce a method statement for the work

C Consult the building occupier

D Check what the ductwork will carry in the future

**25.31** Which of the following do you **not** need to do before cleaning a system in industrial, laboratory or other premises where you might encounter harmful particulates?

A Examine the system

B Collect a sample from the ductwork

C Run the system under overload conditions

D Prepare a job-specific risk assessment and method statement

**25.32** Where it is necessary to enter ductwork, which are the **two** main factors that need to be considered?

A Working in a confined space

B What the ductwork will carry in the future

C The cleanliness of the ductwork

D Whether you need to wear kneepads

E The strength of the ductwork and its supports

**25.33** What should you do before painting the external surface of ductwork?

A Clean the paintbrushes

B Read the COSHH assessment

C Switch off the system

D Put on eye protection

**25.34** What **must** you ensure before using a ladder?

A That it is secured to prevent it from moving sideways or sliding outwards

B That no-one else has booked the ladder for their work

C That an apprentice or workmate is standing by in case you slip and fall

D That the weather forecast is for a bright, clear day

**25.35** When positioning and erecting a stepladder, which of the following is essential for its safe use?

A It has a tool tray towards the top of the steps

B The restraint mechanism is spread to its full extent

C You will be able to reach the job by standing on the top step

D Your supervisor has positioned and erected the steps

**25.36** What is the recommended **maximum** height for a free-standing mobile tower?

A There is no restriction

B 2 m

C The height recommended by the manufacturer

D 12 m

**25.37** What is the **first** thing you should do after getting on to the platform of a correctly erected mobile tower?

A Check that the brakes are locked on

B Check for overhead power lines

C Close the access hatch to prevent falls of personnel, tools or equipment

D Make sure that the tower does not rock or wobble

**25.38** What should be done before a mobile tower is moved?

A All people and equipment must be removed from the platform

B A permit to work must be issued

C The principal contractor must give their approval

D Arrangements must be made with the forklift truck driver

**25.39** What must be done **first** before any roof work is carried out?

A A risk assessment must be carried out

B The operatives working on the roof must be trained in the use of safety harnesses

C Permits to work must be issued only to those allowed to work on the roof

D A weather forecast must be obtained

**25.40** What is edge protection designed to do?

A Make access to the roof easier

B Secure tools and materials close to the edge

C Prevent rainwater running off the roof onto workers below

D Prevent the fall of people and materials

**25.41** When assembling a mobile tower what major hazard **must** you be aware of?

A Water pipes

B Cable trays

C False ceilings

D Overhead service cables

**25.42** What should folding stepladders be used for?

A General access on site

B Short-term works

C All site activities where a straight ladder cannot be used

D Getting on and off mobile towers

**25.43** If you are asked to install high-level ductwork from a platform that has no edge protection and is located above an open stairwell, what should you do?

A Get on with the job, but keep away from the edge of the platform

B Not start work until your work platform has been fitted with guard-rails and toe-boards

C Get on with the job, ensuring that a workmate stays close by

D Get on with the job, provided that if you fall the stairwell guard-rail will prevent you from falling further

**25.44** What is the **best** form of access to use, when installing a run of ceiling-mounted ductwork across a large open space?

A Stepladder

B Metal trestles

C Wooden trestles

D Mobile tower

**25.45** You have to carry out a job over a few days on the flat roof of a two-storey building, about 1 m from the edge of the roof, which has a low parapet. How should you reduce your risk of falling?

A Carry on with the job, provided that you don't get dizzy with heights

B Use a full body harness, lanyard and anchor while doing the job

C Ask for double guard-rails and a toe-board to be installed

D Get your mate to do the work, while you hold on to them

# 26 HVACR – Refrigeration and air conditioning

**26.01** When a new piece of plant has been installed but has **not** been commissioned, how should it be left?

A. With all valves and switches turned off

B. With all valves and switches clearly labelled

C. With all valves and switches locked off

D. With all valves and switches turned on and ready to use

**26.02** When working on refrigeration systems containing hydrocarbon (HC) gases, what particular danger needs to be considered?

A. There should be no sources of ignition

B. Special personal protective equipment (PPE) should be worn to prevent injuries caused by the cold

C. Extra lighting is needed to prevent trips

D. The work cannot be carried out when the weather is hot

**26.03** What should you do when it is necessary to cut into an existing refrigerant pipe?

A. Vent the gas in the pipework to atmosphere

B. Recover the refrigerant gas and make a record of it, then do the work

C. Work on the pipework with the refrigerant gas still in it

D. Not carry out the work at all, because of the risks

**26.04** What is the **first** thing that should be done when a new refrigeration system has been installed?

A. It should be pressure and leak tested

B. It should be filled with refrigerant

C. It should be left open to the air

D. It should be turned off at the electrical switch

**26.05** Which of these statements is **true** of the water in water-cooled systems?

A. It should be replaced annually

B. It should be chemically treated

C. It should be properly filtered

D. It should be drinking water

**26.06** Who is permitted to install, service or maintain systems that contain or are designed to contain refrigerant gases?

A. A Gas Safe registered engineer

B. The person whose plant contains the gas

C. A competent, trained person who works for an F-Gas registered company

D. A fully qualified electrician

**26.07** When working in a riser, how should access be controlled?

A By a site security operative

B By those who are working in it

C By the main contractor

D By a permit to work system

**26.08** If you find a coloured wire sticking out of an electrical plug what is the correct action to take?

A Push it back into the plug and carry on working

B Pull the wire clear of the plug and report it to your supervisor

C Mark the item as defective and follow your company procedure for defective items

D Take the plug apart and carry out a repair

**26.09** How should extension leads in use on site be positioned?

A They should be located so as to prevent a tripping hazard

B They should be laid out in the shortest, most convenient route

C They should be coiled on a drum or cable tidy

D They should be raised on bricks

**26.10** What should you do if you need additional temporary wiring for your power tools whilst working on site?

A Find some cable and extend the wiring yourself

B Stop work until an authorised supply has been installed

C Speak to an electrician and ask them to do the temporary wiring

D Disconnect a longer cable serving somewhere else and reconnect it to where you need it

**26.11** Which item of electrical equipment does **not** require portable appliance testing?

A 110 volt electrical power tool

B Battery-powered rechargeable power tool

C 240 volt electrical power tool

D 240 volt charger for battery-powered tools

**26.12** When repairing an electrically driven compressor, what is the **minimum** safe method of isolation?

A Pressing the stop button

B Pressing the emergency stop button

C Turning off the local isolator

D Locking off and tagging out the local isolator

**26.13** When a refrigerant leak is reported in a closed area, what should you do **first** before entering the area?

A Ventilate the area

B Establish that it is safe to enter

C Get a torch

D Wear safety footwear

**26.14** Where should liquefied petroleum gas (LPG) cylinders be positioned when supplying an appliance in a site cabin?

A Inside the cabin in a locked cupboard

B Under the cabin

C Inside the cabin next to the appliance

D Outside the cabin

**26.15** How should you position the exhaust of an engine-driven generator that has to be run inside a building?

A Outside the building

B In a stairwell

C In another room

D In a riser

**26.16** How should cylinders (full or empty) that contain liquefied petroleum gas (LPG) or acetylene be stored on site?

A In a locked cellar with clear warning signs

B In a locked cage at least 3 m from any oxygen cylinders

C As close to the point of use as possible

D Covered by a tarpaulin to shield the compressed cylinder from sunlight

**26.17** If you spill some oil on the floor and you do **not** have any absorbent material to clean the area, what should you do?

A Spread it about to lessen the depth

B Keep people out of the area and inform your supervisor

C Do nothing, as it will eventually soak into the floor

D Warn other people as they tread through it

**26.18** Where is the **safest** place to store refrigerant cylinders when they are **not** in use?

A Outside in a special locked storage compound

B In a company vehicle

C Inside the building in a locked cupboard

D In the immediate work area, ready for use the next day

**26.19** If refrigerant gases are released into a closed room in a building, what would they do?

A Sink to the floor

B Rise to the ceiling

C Stay at the same level

D Disperse safely within the room

**26.20** If you have to drill through a wall panel that you suspect contains an asbestos material, what should you do?

A Ignore it and carry on

B Put on safety goggles

C Put on a dust mask

D Stop work and report it

**26.21** When using a van to transport a refrigerant bottle, how should it be carried?

A In the back of the van

B In the passenger footwell of the van

C In a purpose-built container within the rear of the van, with appropriate signage

D In the van with all the windows open

**26.22** What safety devices should be fitted between the pipes and the gauges of oxyacetylene brazing equipment?

A Non-return valves

B On-off taps

C Flame retardant tape

D Flashback arresters

**26.23** Why is it essential to take great care when handling oxygen cylinders?

A They contain highly flammable compressed gas

B They contain highly flammable liquid gas

C They are filled to extremely high pressures

D They contain poisonous gas

**26.24** If you are working where welding is being carried out, what should be provided to protect you from welding flash?

A A fire extinguisher

B Warning notices

C Screens

D A hi-vis vest

**26.25** When using a blowtorch or brazing equipment to joint copper tube and fittings in a property, how should a fire extinguisher be made available?

- (A) It should be available in the immediate work area
- (B) It should be held over the joint while you are using the blowtorch
- (C) It should be used to cool the fitting
- (D) It should be available only if a property is occupied

**26.26** If you are carrying out hot works with a blowtorch, when should you stop using it?

- (A) Just before you leave the site
- (B) At least one hour before you leave the site
- (C) At least two hours before you leave the site
- (D) At least four hours before you leave the site

**26.27** Why must you **never** use oxygen when pressure testing?

- (A) The molecules of the gas are too small
- (B) The pressure required would not be reached
- (C) When oxygen meets oil in a compressor it could explode and cause serious injury or death
- (D) There is too much temperature pressure difference and a true record will not be given

**26.28** What should you ensure when pressure testing with nitrogen?

- (A) That the nitrogen bottle is laid down to avoid it falling over
- (B) That the nitrogen gauge can take the pressure required and that the bottle is secured upright
- (C) That the temperature of the bottle is at room temperature to avoid a temperature pressure difference
- (D) That purge brazing has taken place during the installation

**26.29** When planning a lifting operation how should the sequence of operations to enable a safe lift be confirmed?

- (A) By verbal instruction
- (B) In a method statement
- (C) In a radio telephone message
- (D) Via a notice in the canteen

**26.30** Which of these statements is **true** in relation to the SWL of lifting equipment?

- (A) It is never marked on the equipment but kept with the test certificates
- (B) It is provided for guidance only
- (C) It may be exceeded by no more than 25%
- (D) It is the absolute maximum safe working load

**26.31** What **must** be clearly marked on all lifting equipment?

A The name of the manufacturer

B The safe working load

C The next test date

D The specification of material from which it is made

**26.32** Which of these items of personal protective equipment (PPE) is designed to protect against infrared radiation damage to the eyes during flame cutting or welding?

A Respiratory protective equipment

B Clear goggles

C Eye protection with a tinted filter lens

D Dust mask

**26.33** How should you position the bottles when using oxyacetylene brazing equipment?

A Laid on their side and secured

B Stood upright and secured

C Stood upside down

D Angled at 45°

**26.34** Which **two** of the following are essential safety checks that need to be carried out before using oxyacetylene equipment?

A That the cylinders are full

B That the cylinders, hoses and flashback arresters are in good condition

C That the trolley wheels are the right size

D That the area is well ventilated and clear of any obstructions

E That the cylinders are the right weight

**26.35** When handling refrigerant gases, what personal protective equipment (PPE) should you wear as a **minimum**?

A Eye protection, overalls, thermal-resistant gloves and helmet

B Eye protection, overalls, thermal-resistant gloves and safety boots

C Eye protection, overalls, harness and safety boots

D Overalls, thermal-resistant gloves, helmet and safety boots

**26.36** What should you establish before entering a cold room?

A The size of the cold room

B The temperature of the cold room

C Whether the exit door is fitted with an internal handle

D Whether there are lights and power in the cold room

**26.37** What **must** you ensure before using a ladder?

A. That it is secured to prevent it from moving sideways or sliding outwards

B. That no-one else has booked the ladder for their work

C. That an apprentice or workmate is standing by in case you slip and fall

D. That the weather forecast is for a bright, clear day

**26.38** When positioning and erecting a stepladder, which of the following is essential for its safe use?

A. It has a tool tray towards the top of the steps

B. The restraint mechanism is spread to its full extent

C. You will be able to reach the job by standing on the top step

D. Your supervisor has positioned and erected the steps

**26.39** What is the recommended **maximum** height for a free-standing mobile tower?

A. There is no restriction

B. 2 m

C. The height recommended by the manufacturer

D. 12 m

**26.40** What is the **first** thing you should do after getting on to the platform of a correctly erected mobile tower?

A. Check that the brakes are locked on

B. Check for overhead power lines

C. Close the access hatch to prevent falls of personnel, tools or equipment

D. Make sure that the tower does not rock or wobble

**26.41** What should be done before a mobile tower is moved?

A. All people and equipment must be removed from the platform

B. A permit to work must be issued

C. The principal contractor must give their approval

D. Arrangements must be made with the forklift truck driver

**26.42** What must be done **first** before any roof work is carried out?

A. A risk assessment must be carried out

B. The operatives working on the roof must be trained in the use of safety harnesses

C. Permits to work must be issued only to those allowed to work on the roof

D. A weather forecast must be obtained

**26.43** What is edge protection designed to do?

A Make access to the roof easier

B Secure tools and materials close to the edge

C Prevent rainwater running off the roof onto workers below

D Prevent the fall of people and materials

**26.44** When assembling a mobile tower what major hazard **must** you be aware of?

A Water pipes

B Cable trays

C False ceilings

D Overhead service cables

**26.45** You have to carry out a job, over a few days, on the flat roof of a two-storey building, about 1 m from the edge of the roof, which has a low parapet. How should you reduce your risk of falling?

A Carry on with the job, provided you don't get dizzy with heights

B Use a full body harness, lanyard and anchor while doing the job

C Ask for double guard-rails and toe-boards to be installed to prevent you falling

D Get your mate to do the work, while you hold on to them

**26.46** You have been asked to install a number of ceiling-mounted air-conditioning units in a large, open-plan area, which has a good floor. What is the **best** way to access the work area?

A From a stepladder

B From scaffold boards and floor stands

C By standing on packing cases

D From a mobile tower

# 27 HVACR – Services and facilities maintenance

**27.01** When arriving at an occupied building, who or what should you consult to find out about any asbestos in the premises before starting work?

A The person responsible for the building, so you can view the asbestos register

B The building's receptionist

C The building's logbook

D The building's caretaker

**27.02** Where might you find information on the safe way to maintain the services in a building?

A The noticeboard

B The safety officer

C The local Health and Safety Executive (HSE) office

D The health and safety file for the building

**27.03** In the normal office environment what should be the hot water temperature at the tap furthest from the boiler, after it has been run for one minute?

A At least 15°C

B At least 35°C

C At least 50°C

D At least 100°C

**27.04** What should be the **maximum** temperature for a cold water supply, after it has been run for one minute?

A 10°C

B 20°C

C 35°C

D 50°C

**27.05** What is required if there is a cooling tower on site?

A A formal logbook

B A written scheme of examination

C Regular visits by the Local Authority Environmental Health officer

D Inspections by the water supplier

**27.06** Which **two** of the following are pressure systems?

A Medium and high temperature hot water systems at or above 95°C

B Cold water systems

C Steam systems

D Office tea urns

E Domestic heating systems

**27.07** What is required before a pressure system can be operated?

A. A written scheme of examination

B. A hot-work permit

C. Operative certification

D. A minimum of two competent persons to operate the system

**27.08** Which of these statements is **true** in relation to the water used in cooling systems?

A. It should be replaced annually

B. It should be chemically treated

C. It should be chilled

D. It should be drinking water

**27.09** Which of the following should you **not** do when replacing the filters in an air-conditioning system?

A. Put the old filters in a dustbin

B. Follow a job-specific risk assessment and method statement

C. Wear appropriate overalls

D. Wear a respirator

**27.10** After servicing a gas boiler, what checks **must** you make by law?

A. Check for water leaks

B. Check for flueing, ventilation, gas rate and safe functioning

C. Check the pressure relief valve

D. Check the thermostat setting

**27.11** What **must** you do before adding inhibitor to a heating system?

A. Check for leaks on the system

B. Raise the system to working temperature

C. Read the COSHH assessment for the product

D. Bleed the heat emitters

**27.12** How should access to a riser be controlled?

A. By a site security operative

B. By those who are working in it

C. By the main contractor

D. By a permit to work system

**27.13** What is the correct action to take if natural gas is detected in an underground service duct?

A No action, as it is not harmful

B Evacuate the duct

C Carry on working but do not use electrical equipment

D Carry on working until the end of the shift

**27.14** What should you consider **first** when planning to work in a confined space?

A Whether the job has been priced properly

B Whether sufficient resource has been allocated

C Whether the correct tools have been arranged

D Whether the work could be done in another way to avoid the need to enter the confined space

**27.15** How should an adequate supply of breathable fresh air be provided in a confined space when breathing apparatus is **not** being worn?

A An opening in the top of the confined space

B Forced mechanical ventilation

C Natural ventilation

D An opening at the bottom of the confined space

**27.16** What are the **two** main safety considerations when using oxyacetylene equipment in a confined space?

A The hoses may not be long enough

B Unburnt oxygen may cause an oxygen-enriched atmosphere

C The burner will be hard to light

D Wearing the correct goggles

E The risk of a flammable gas leak

**27.17** What precaution should be taken to protect against lighting failure in a confined space?

A Remember where you got in

B Ensure it is daylight when you do the work

C Each operative should carry a torch

D Secure a rope near the entrance and trail it behind you so that you can trace your way back

**27.18** While working on your own and tracing pipework in a building, you notice that the pipes enter a service duct. What should you do?

A Go into the service duct and continue to trace the pipework

B Ask someone in the building to act as your second person

C Put on your personal protective equipment (PPE) and carry on with the job

D Stop work until a risk assessment has been carried out

**27.19** Before working on electrically powered equipment, what is the procedure to make sure that the supply is dead before work starts?

A Switch off and remove the fuses

B Switch off and cut through the supply with insulated pliers

C Test the circuit, switch off and isolate the supply at the mains board

D Switch off, isolate the supply at the mains board, lock out and tag

**27.20** What would you use to find out whether a wall into which you are about to drill contains an electric supply?

A A neon screwdriver

B A cable tracer

C A multimeter

D A hammer and chisel

**27.21** Which type of power drill is **most** suitable for fixing a run of pipework outside in wet weather?

A Battery-powered drill

B Drill with 110 volt power supply

C Drill with 24 volt power supply

D Any mains voltage drill with a power breaker

**27.22** Why is temporary continuity bonding carried out before removing and replacing sections of metallic pipework?

A To provide a continuous earth for the pipework installation

B To prevent any chance of blowing a fuse

C To maintain the live supply to the electrical circuit

D To prevent any chance of corrosion to the pipework

**27.23** What is the procedure for ensuring that the electrical supply is dead before replacing an electric immersion heater?

A Switch off and disconnect the supply to the immersion heater

B Switch off and cut through the electric cable with insulated pliers

C Switch off and test the circuit

D Lock off the supply, isolate at the mains board, test the circuit and hang a warning sign

**27.24** What is used to reduce 230 volts to 110 volts on site?

A RCD (residual current device)

B Transformer

C Circuit breaker

D Step-down generator

**27.25** What colour power outlet on a portable generator would supply 230 volts?

A Black

B Blue

C Red

D Yellow

**27.26** What action should you take if a natural gas leak is reported in a closed area?

A Ventilate the area and phone the gas emergency service

B Establish whether or not it is safe to enter

C Turn off the light

D Wear safety footwear

**27.27** Which of the following actions should you take if a refrigerant leak is reported in a closed area?

A Switch off the system, ventilate the area and test to establish if it is safe to enter

B Trace the leak and try to make a temporary repair

C Leave the system running until all of the gas has leaked out and then make a repair

D No action is required, as refrigerant gas is completely harmless

**27.28** How is legionella transmitted?

A By breathing contaminated airborne water droplets

B Through human contact

C Through contact with dirty clothes

D Via rat urine

**27.29** What is the ideal temperature for legionella to breed?

Between 75°C and 100°C

Between 45°C and 75°C

Between 20°C and 45°C

Below 20°C

**27.30** Which of the following is the **most** likely place to find legionella?

A In drinking water

B In hot water taps above 50°C

C In infrequently used shower heads

D In a river

F 27

**27.31** When assembling a mobile access tower what major hazard **must** you be aware of?

A Water pipes

B Cable trays

C False ceilings

D Overhead service cables

**27.32** If you spill some oil on the floor and you do **not** have any absorbent material to clean the area, what should you do?

A Spread it about to lessen the depth

B Keep people out of the area and inform your supervisor

C Do nothing, as it will eventually soak into the floor

D Warn other people as they tread through it

**27.33** How should liquefied petroleum gas (LPG) cylinders be carried to and from premises in a van?

A In the back of the van

B In the passenger footwell of the van

C In a purpose-built container within the rear of the van, with appropriate signage

D In the van with all the windows open

**27.34** When removing some panelling, you see a section of cabling with the wires showing. What should you do?

A Carry on with your work, trying your best to avoid the cables

B Touch the cables to see if they are live, and if so refuse to carry out the work

C Wrap the defective cable with approved electrical insulation tape

D Only work when the cable has been isolated or repaired by a competent person

**27.35** When **must** a shaft or pit be securely covered or have double guard-rails and toe-boards installed?

A At a fall height of 1 m

B When there is a potential risk of anyone falling into it

C At a fall height of 2.5 m

D At a fall height of 3 m

**27.36** What should you do if, when carrying out a particular task, the correct tool is **not** available?

A Wait until you have the appropriate tool for the task

B Borrow a tool from the building caretaker

C Use the best tool available in the toolkit

D Modify one of the tools you have

**27.37** Who should be informed if a legionella outbreak is suspected?

A The Health and Safety Executive (HSE)

B The police

C A coroner

D The nearest hospital

**27.38** When should the use of a permit to work be considered?

A For all high risk work activities

B For all equipment isolations

C At the beginning of each shift

D When there is enough time to complete the paperwork

**27.39** Who should fit a padlock and tag to an electrical lock-out guard?

A Anyone working on the system

B Only the person who fitted the lock-out guard

C The senior engineer

D The site supervisor

**27.40** If you arrive on site and find the mains isolator for a component is switched off, what should you do?

A Switch it on and get on with your work

B Switch it on and check the safety circuits to see if there is a fault

C Contact the person in control of the premises

D Ask people around the building and, if no-one responds, switch it on and get on with your work

**27.41** When carrying out solvent welding on plastic pipework, what particular safety measure **must** you apply?

A The area must be well ventilated

B The supervisor must be present

C The area must be enclosed

D It must be done in daylight

**27.42** Before starting work on a particular piece of equipment, who or what should you consult?

A The machine brochure

B The operation and maintenance manual for the equipment

C The manufacturer's data plate

D The store person

**27.43** Which **two** of the following should a person who is going to work alone carry out to ensure their safety?

A Register their presence with the site representative before starting work

B Ensure their timesheet is accurate and countersigned

C Make sure that somebody regularly checks that they are OK

D Notify the site manager of the details of the work

E Only work outside of normal working hours

**27.44** What **must** you ensure to prevent unauthorised access to an unoccupied plant or switchgear room?

A That the access door is locked

B That a sign is posted

C That the power supply is isolated

D That a person is posted to prevent access

**27.45** What should folding stepladders be used for?

A General access on site

B Short-term work

C All site activities where a straight ladder cannot be used

D Getting on and off mobile towers

**27.46** When positioning and erecting a stepladder, which of the following is essential for its safe use?

A It has a tool tray towards the top of the steps

B The restraint mechanism is spread to its full extent

C You will be able to reach the job by standing on the top step

D Your supervisor has positioned and erected the steps

**27.47** What is the **first** thing you should do after getting on to the platform of a correctly erected mobile tower?

A Check that the brakes are locked on

B Check for overhead power lines

C Close the access hatch to prevent falls of personnel, tools or equipment

D Make sure that the tower does not rock or wobble

# 28 Plumbing (JIB)

**28.01** What should you do when using a blowtorch near to flexible pipe lagging?

A. Remove just enough lagging to carry out the work

B. Remove the lagging at least 1 m either side of the work

C. Remove the lagging at least 3 m either side of the work

D. Wet the lagging but leave it in place

**28.02** What is the **most** likely risk of injury when cutting large diameter pipe?

A. Your fingers may become trapped between the cutting wheel and the pipe

B. You may cut yourself on the inside edge of the cut pipe

C. You may damage your muscles due to continued use

D. A piece of sharp metal could fly off and hit you

**28.03** If you have been handling sheet lead, what is the **most** likely way lead could get into your bloodstream?

A. By not using the correct respirator

B. By not washing your hands before eating

C. By not changing out of your work clothes

D. By not wearing safety goggles

**28.04** The legionella bacteria that cause legionnaires' disease are **most** likely to be found in which of the following?

A. A boiler operating at a temperature of 80°C

B. A shower hose outlet

C. A cold water storage cistern containing water at 10°C

D. A toilet pan

**28.05** How are legionella bacteria passed on to humans?

A. Through fine water droplets, such as sprays or mists

B. By drinking dirty water

C. Through contact with the skin

D. From other people when they sneeze

**28.06** Which item of PPE is designed to protect against infrared radiation damage to the eyes during flame cutting or welding?

A. Impact-rated safety goggles

B. Respiratory protective equipment

C. Reflective vest

D. Eye protection with a tinted or filter lens

**28.07** If you are drilling a hole, when do you need to wear eye protection?

A Only when drilling overhead

B Only when the drill bit exceeds 20 mm

C Always, whatever the circumstances

D Only when drilling through concrete

**28.08** What should you do when repairing a burst water main using pipe-freezing equipment to isolate the damaged section of pipe?

A Always work in pairs when using pipe-freezing equipment

B Never allow the freezing gas to come into direct contact with surface water

C Never use pipe-freezing equipment on plastic pipe

D Wear gloves to avoid direct contact with the skin

**28.09** You are drilling a 100 mm diameter hole for a flue pipe through a brick wall with a large hammer drill. Which combination of personal protective equipment (PPE) should you be supplied with?

A Gloves, breathing apparatus and ear defenders

B Ear defenders, respiratory protective equipment and eye protection

C Ear defenders, respiratory protective equipment and barrier cream

D Barrier cream, boots and respiratory protective equipment

**28.10** While working, you come across a hard, white, powdery material that could be asbestos. What should you do?

A While wearing respiratory protective equipment, remove the material and dispose of it safely

B Remove the material, putting it back after finishing the job

C Stop work immediately and tell your supervisor about the material

D Dampen the material down with water and remove it before carrying out the work

**28.11** Why is it important that operatives know the difference between propane and butane equipment?

A Propane equipment operates at higher pressure

B Propane equipment operates at lower pressure

C Propane equipment is cheaper

D Propane equipment can be used with smaller, easy-to-handle cylinders

**28.12** Which of the following statements is **true**?

A Both propane and butane are heavier than air

B Butane is heavier than air while propane is lighter than air

C Propane is heavier than air while butane is lighter than air

D Both propane and butane are lighter than air

**28.13** Apart from the cylinders used in gas-powered forklift trucks, why should liquefied petroleum gas (LPG) cylinders **never** be placed on their side during use?

A) It would give a faulty reading on the contents gauge, resulting in flashback

B) Air could be drawn into the cylinder, creating a dangerous mixture of gases

C) The liquid gas would be at too low a level to allow the torch to burn correctly

D) The liquid gas could be drawn from the cylinder, creating a safety hazard

**28.14** What is the preferred method of checking for leaks when assembling liquefied petroleum gas (LPG) equipment before use?

A) Test with a lighted match

B) Sniff the connections to detect the smell of gas

C) Listen to hear for escaping gas

D) Apply leak detection fluid to the connections

**28.15** The use of oxyacetylene equipment is **not** recommended for which of the following jointing methods?

A) Jointing copper pipe using hard soldering

B) Jointing copper tube using capillary soldered fittings

C) Jointing mild steel tube

D) Jointing sheet lead

**28.16** Which of the following makes it essential to take great care when handling and transporting oxygen cylinders?

A) They contain highly flammable compressed gas

B) They contain highly flammable liquid gas

C) They are filled to extremely high pressures

D) They contain poisonous gas

**28.17** Where is the **safest** place to store oxyacetylene gas-welding bottles when they are **not** in use?

A) Outside in a special storage compound

B) In company vehicles

C) Inside the building in a locked cupboard

D) In the immediate work area, ready for use the next day

**28.18** Where should a fire extinguisher be if you are using a blowtorch to joint copper tube and fittings in a domestic property?

A) Available in the immediate work area

B) In your vehicle, as long as the doors are locked

C) There is no need for a fire extinguisher

D) Available only if a property is occupied

**28.19** What should you do if you are using a blowtorch near to timber?

A Carry out the work taking care not to catch the timber

B Use a non-combustible mat and have a fire extinguisher ready

C Wet the timber first and have a bucket of water handy

D Point the flame away from the timber and have a bucket of sand ready to put out the fire

**28.20** What is the colour of an acetylene cylinder?

A Orange

B Black

C Green

D Maroon

**28.21** How should bottles be positioned when using oxyacetylene welding equipment?

A Laid on their side and secured

B Stood upright and secured

C Stood upside down

D Angled at 45°

**28.22** You are required to replace below-ground drainage pipework in an excavation, which is approximately 2.5 m deep, but the trench sides show signs of collapse. What should you do?

A Get on with the work as quickly as possible

B Refuse to do the work until the trench sides have been properly supported

C Get a mate to help you so that they can pass the materials down to you

D Ensure that you do the work with a rope around you so that you can be pulled out

**28.23** You are working in an occupied building and have taken up six lengths of 3 m floor boarding when you are called away to an urgent job. What should you do?

A Leave the job as it is

B Cordon off the work area before leaving the job

C Permanently re-fix the floorboards and floor coverings

D Tell other workers to be careful while you are away

**28.24** You are preparing to use an electric-powered threading machine. Which of the following statements should apply?

A The power supply should be 24 volts and the machine fitted with a guard

B The power supply should be 400 volts and the machine fitted with a guard

C Ensure your clothing cannot get caught on rotating parts of the machine

D Ear defenders should be available and should be in good condition

**28.25** When replacing an electrical immersion heater in a hot water storage cylinder, what should you do to make sure that the electrical supply is dead before starting plumbing work?

A. Switch off and disconnect the supply to the immersion heater

B. Switch off and cut through the electric cable with insulated pliers

C. Switch off and test the circuit

D. Switch off, isolate the supply at the mains board and test the circuit

**28.26** Why should you carry out temporary continuity bonding before removing and replacing sections of metallic pipework?

A. To provide a continuous earth for the pipework installation

B. To prevent any chance of blowing a fuse

C. To maintain the live supply to the electrical circuit

D. To prevent any chance of corrosion to the pipework

**28.27** If you are required to re-fix a section of external rainwater pipe using a power drill in wet weather conditions, which type of drill is **most** suitable?

A. Battery-powered drill

B. Drill with 110 volt power supply

C. Drill with 240 volt power supply

D. Any mains voltage drill with a power breaker

**28.28** What piece of equipment would you use to find out whether a section of solid wall that you are about to drill into contains electric cables?

A. A neon screwdriver

B. A cable tracer

C. A multimeter

D. A hammer and chisel

**28.29** When is it safe to transport workers to the workplace in the rear of a van?

A. When the driver has a heavy goods vehicle licence

B. When the van is fitted with temporary seating

C. When the van is fitted with proper seating and seat belts

D. When the driver is over 21 years of age

**28.30** Which is the **safest** method of transporting long lengths of copper pipe by van?

A. Tying the pipes to the roof with copper wire

B. Someone holding the pipes on the roof rack as you drive along

C. Putting the pipes inside the van with the ends out of the passenger window

D. Using a pipe rack fixed to the roof of the van

**28.31** If lifting a roll of Code 5 sheet lead, what is the **first** thing you should do?

A Weigh the roll of lead

B Have a trial lift to see how heavy it feels

C Assess the whole task

D Ask your workmate to give you a hand

**28.32** What should you do if you need to move a cast iron bath, but it is too heavy to lift by yourself?

A Inform your supervisor and ask for assistance

B Get a lifting accessory

C Give it another try

D Try and find someone to give you a hand

**28.33** How should you install a flue into an existing chimney?

A Insert the liner from roof level using a roof ladder

B Work in pairs and insert the liner from roof level, working off the roof

C Work in pairs and insert the liner from roof level, working from a chimney scaffold

D Break through the chimney in the loft area and insert the liner from there

**28.34** If you are asked to move a cast iron boiler some distance, what should you do?

A Get a workmate to carry it

B Drag it

C Roll it end-over-end

D Use a suitable trolley or other manual handling aid

**28.35** If working on a plumbing job where noise levels are rather high, who would you expect to carry out noise assessment?

A A fully qualified plumber

B Your supervisor

C The site engineer

D A competent person

**28.36** You are protected from falls from height when fixing sheet lead flashing to a chimney on the roof of a busy town centre shop. What is the **most** important thing you **must** do?

A Pull the ladder onto the roof to prevent the public from climbing up

B Make provision for protecting the public from objects that could fall

C Wear a face mask to protect you from breathing the chimney fumes

D Wear safety boots to prevent you from slipping off the roof

**28.37** You are removing guttering from a large, single-storey, metal-framed and cladded building and the job is likely to take all day. What is the **most** appropriate type of access equipment you could use?

A. A ladder

B. A mobile access tower

C. A putlog scaffold

D. A trestle scaffold

**28.38** What should you do if you arrive at a job which involves using ladder access to the roof and you notice that the ladder has been painted?

A. Only use the ladder if it is made of metal

B. Only use the ladder if it is made of wood

C. Only use the ladder if wearing rubber-soled boots to prevent slipping

D. Not use the ladder, and report the matter to your supervisor

# Further information

## Contents

## 01 General responsibilities

| Question | Answer |
|---|---|
| 1.01 | D |
| 1.02 | B |
| 1.03 | B |
| 1.04 | A |
| 1.05 | B |
| 1.06 | Site office → / Site office 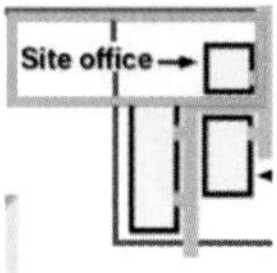 |
| 1.07 | B |
| 1.08 | C, E |
| 1.09 | D |
| 1.10 | C |
| 1.11 | C, E |
| 1.12 | C |
| 1.13 | C |
| 1.14 | D |
| 1.15 | C |
| 1.16 | A |
| 1.17 | A, D |
| 1.18 | C |
| 1.19 | B |
| 1.20 | B |
| 1.21 | A |
| 1.22 | A, C |
| 1.23 | C |
| 1.24 | A |
| 1.25 | C |
| 1.26 | B, D |

## 02 Accident reporting and recording

| Question | Answer |
|---|---|
| 2.01 | B, D |
| 2.02 | A, E |
| 2.03 | C |
| 2.04 | C |
| 2.05 | B |
| 2.06 | C |
| 2.07 | A |
| 2.08 | B |
| 2.09 | A |
| 2.10 | C |
| 2.11 | A |
| 2.12 | B, D |
| 2.13 | A |
| 2.14 | C |
| 2.15 | B |
| 2.16 | D |

## 02 Accident reporting and recording (continued)

| | |
|---|---|
| 2.17 | D |
| 2.18 | C |
| 2.19 | B |
| 2.20 | D |
| 2.21 | C |
| 2.22 | B |
| 2.23 | A, D |
| 2.24 | C |
| 2.25 | D |
| 2.26 | B |
| 2.27 | B |

## 03 Health and welfare

| | | | |
|---|---|---|---|
| 3.01 | C | 3.12 | A |
| 3.02 | D | 3.13 | C |
| 3.03 | Welfare facilities | 3.14 | B |
| | | 3.15 | D |
| | | 3.16 | A |
| | | 3.17 | D |
| 3.04 | B | 3.18 | A |
| 3.05 | C | 3.19 | B |
| 3.06 | A, B | 3.20 | Needles |
| 3.07 | A | | |
| 3.08 | A | | |
| 3.09 | B | | |
| 3.10 | D | 3.21 | B |
| 3.11 | B | | |

## 04 First aid and emergency procedures

| | | | |
|---|---|---|---|
| 4.01 | C | 4.09 | C |
| 4.02 | A, E | 4.10 | D |
| 4.03 | D | 4.11 | C |
| 4.04 | C | 4.12 | D |
| 4.05 | A | 4.13 | C |
| 4.06 | B | 4.14 | B |
| 4.07 | B | 4.15 | C |
| 4.08 | C | | |

## 05 Personal protective equipment

| | | | |
|---|---|---|---|
| 5.01 | D | 5.12 | D |
| 5.02 | A | 5.13 | B |
| 5.03 | C | 5.14 | B |
| 5.04 | C | 5.15 | D |
| 5.05 | A | 5.16 | D |
| 5.06 | C | 5.17 | A |
| 5.07 | A | 5.18 | B |
| 5.08 | C | 5.19 | B |
| 5.09 | C | 5.20 | A |
| 5.10 | D | 5.21 | C |
| 5.11 | D | | |

## 06 Dust and fumes (Respiratory hazards)

| | | | |
|---|---|---|---|
| 6.01 | D | 6.12 | D |
| 6.02 | B | 6.13 | B |
| 6.03 | B, C | 6.14 | B |
| 6.04 | B | 6.15 | A |
| 6.05 | C | 6.16 | A, B |
| 6.06 | A | 6.17 | D |
| 6.07 | C | 6.18 | A |
| 6.08 | B | 6.19 | C |
| 6.09 | B | 6.20 | A, D |
| 6.10 | D | 6.21 | B |
| 6.11 | A | 6.22 | D |

## 07 Noise and vibration

| | |
|---|---|
| 7.01 | B |
| 7.02 | A, C |
| 7.03 | A |
| 7.04 | C |
| 7.05 | D |
| 7.06 | B |
| 7.07 | C, E |
| 7.08 | C |
| 7.09 | C |
| 7.10 | 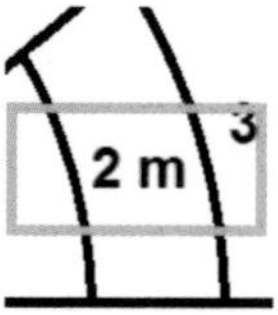 2 m, 3, 2 m |
| 7.11 | C |
| 7.12 | B |
| 7.13 | D |
| 7.14 | D |
| 7.15 | D |
| 7.16 | A, B, D |
| 7.17 | C |
| 7.18 | B |
| 7.19 | C |
| 7.20 | B |
| 7.21 | A |
| 7.22 | B |
| 7.23 | Hand-arm 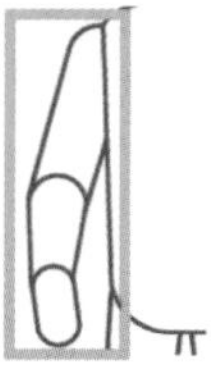 |

## 08 Hazardous substances

| | |
|---|---|
| 8.01 | B |
| 8.02 | C |
| 8.03 | C |
| 8.04 | D |
| 8.05 | B |
| 8.06 | A |
| 8.07 | A, B, C |
| 8.08 | B |
| 8.09 | C |
| 8.10 | C |
| 8.11 | C |
| 8.12 | C |
| 8.13 | C |

## 08 Hazardous substances (continued)

| Question | Answer |
|---|---|
| 8.14 | 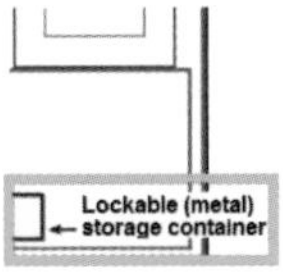 Lockable (metal) storage container |
| 8.15 | D |
| 8.16 | B |
| 8.17 | A |
| 8.18 | A |
| 8.19 | A |
| 8.20 | D |
| 8.21 | B |
| 8.22 | C |
| 8.23 | D |

## 09 Manual handling

| Question | Answer |
|---|---|
| 9.01 | C |
| 9.02 | B |
| 9.03 | A |
| 9.04 | Back 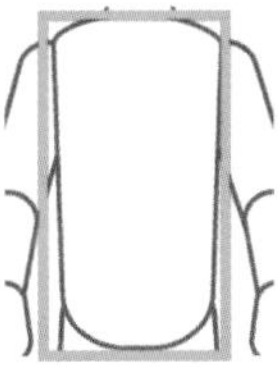 |
| 9.05 | Back 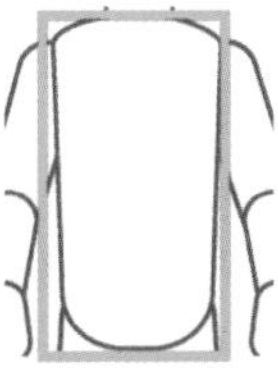 |
| 9.06 | D |
| 9.07 | C |
| 9.08 | A, B, C |
| 9.09 | C, E |
| 9.10 | B |
| 9.11 | A, B, C |
| 9.12 | A |
| 9.13 | A, B |
| 9.14 | D |
| 9.15 | A |
| 9.16 | C |
| 9.17 | C |
| 9.18 | B |
| 9.19 | C |
| 9.20 | A |
| 9.21 | C |
| 9.22 | A |
| 9.23 | A |
| 9.24 | A |
| 9.25 | A |

# 10 Safety signs

| | |
|---|---|
| 10.01 | A |
| 10.02 | B |
| 10.03 | D |
| 10.04 | A |
| 10.05 | D |
| 10.06 | C |
| 10.07 | C |
| 10.08 | B |
| 10.09 | C |
| 10.10 | C |
| 10.11 | C |
| 10.12 | B |
| 10.13 | A |
| 10.14 | B |
| 10.15 | D |
| 10.16 | C |
| 10.17 | C |
| 10.18 | A |
| 10.19 | D |
| 10.20 | D |
| 10.21 | B |
| 10.22 | C |
| 10.23 | A |
| 10.24 | B |
| 10.25 | A |
| 10.26 | B |
| 10.27 | Pedestrian entrance |
| 10.28 | B |
| 10.29 | B |
| 10.30 | D |
| 10.31 | B |
| 10.32 | A |
| 10.33 | B |
| 10.34 | B |
| 10.35 | B |
| 10.36 | C |
| 10.37 | Toxic<br>Harmful to the environment<br>Corrosive<br>Flammable |
| 10.38 | Mandatory<br>Warning<br>Prohibition<br>Safe condition |
| 10.39 | C |

## 10 Safety signs (continued)

10.40
Prohibition 
Mandatory 
Safe condition 
Warning

10.41
Prohibition 
Mandatory 
Safe condition 
Warning

10.42
Prohibition 
Mandatory 
Safe condition 
Warning

10.43
Prohibition 
Mandatory 
Safe condition 
Warning

10.44
Prohibition 
Mandatory 
Safe condition 
Warning

10.45
Prohibition 
Mandatory 
Safe condition 
Warning

10.46
Prohibition 
Mandatory 
Safe condition 
Warning

## 11 Fire prevention and control

| | | | |
|---|---|---|---|
| 11.01 | B, D | 11.08 | A |
| 11.02 | C | 11.09 | C |
| 11.03 | C, E | 11.10 | B, C |
| 11.04 | B | 11.11 | A, B |
| 11.05 | D | 11.12 | A, E |
| 11.06 | B | 11.13 | C |
| 11.07 | C | | |

## 12 Electrical safety, tools and equipment

| | | | |
|---|---|---|---|
| 12.01 | A, C | 12.17 | C, E |
| 12.02 | B, D | 12.18 | D |
| 12.03 | A | 12.19 | B, C, D |
| 12.04 | C | 12.20 | A, C, D |
| 12.05 | B, D | 12.21 | D |
| 12.06 | C | 12.22 | C |
| 12.07 | C | 12.23 | B, D |
| 12.08 | A | 12.24 | D |
| 12.09 | A | 12.25 | A |
| 12.10 | A, E | 12.26 | A |
| 12.11 | C | 12.27 | C |
| 12.12 | D, E | 12.28 | B |
| 12.13 | B | 12.29 | C |
| 12.14 | C | 12.30 | B |
| 12.15 | B | 12.31 | D |
| 12.16 | B | 12.32 | B |

## 12 Electrical safety, tools and equipment (continued)

| | |
|---|---|
| 12.33 | B |
| 12.34 | C |
| 12.35 | B |
| 12.36 | B |
| 12.37 | C |
| 12.38 | A |

## 13 Site transport safety and lifting operations

| | |
|---|---|
| 13.01 | A, B |
| 13.02 | B |
| 13.03 | A |
| 13.04 | C |
| 13.05 | A |
| 13.06 | B |
| 13.07 | C |
| 13.08 | C |
| 13.09 | C |
| 13.10 | D |
| 13.11 | A |
| 13.12 | B |
| 13.13 | D |
| 13.14 | D |
| 13.15 | C |
| 13.16 | D |
| 13.17 | A |
| 13.18 | C |
| 13.19 | D |
| 13.20 | B |
| 13.21 | A |
| 13.22 | D |
| 13.23 | B |
| 13.24 | A |
| 13.25 | B |

## 14 Working at height

| Question | Answer |
|---|---|
| 14.01 | A |
| 14.02 | A, B |
| 14.03 | C |
| 14.04 | C |
| 14.05 | C |
| 14.06 | C |
| 14.07 | D |
| 14.08 | 75° |
| 14.09 | A |
| 14.10 | A |
| 14.11 | A |
| 14.12 | D |
| 14.13 | A |
| 14.14 | A |
| 14.15 | C |
| 14.16 | B |
| 14.17 | B |
| 14.18 | A |
| 14.19 | C |
| 14.20 | A |
| 14.21 | B |
| 14.22 | D |
| 14.23 | B |
| 14.24 | A |
| 14.25 | D |
| 14.26 | C |
| 14.27 | B |
| 14.28 | C |
| 14.29 | C |
| 14.30 | D |
| 14.31 | B |
| 14.32 | C |
| 14.33 | A |

## 15 Excavations and confined spaces

| Question | Answer |
|---|---|
| 15.01 | B |
| 15.02 | C |
| 15.03 | B |
| 15.04 | D |
| 15.05 | B |
| 15.06 | B |
| 15.07 | A |
| 15.08 | D |
| 15.09 | C |
| 15.10 | C |

## 15 Excavations and confined spaces (continued)

| | |
|---|---|
| 15.11 | B |
| 15.12 | C |
| 15.13 | B |
| 15.14 | B |
| 15.15 | A, E |
| 15.16 | C |
| 15.17 | A, D, E |
| 15.18 | A |
| 15.19 | D |
| 15.20 | D |
| 15.21 | B |
| 15.22 | B |
| 15.23 | B |
| 15.24 | B |
| 15.25 | C |

# 16 Environmental awareness and waste control

| | |
|---|---|
| 16.01 | D |
| 16.02 | A, C, E |
| 16.03 | A, D |
| 16.04 | B |
| 16.05 | A, D |
| 16.06 | D |
| 16.07 | B, D |
| 16.08 | D, E |
| 16.09 | Broken bricks: Non-hazardous<br>Timber off-cuts: Non-hazardous<br>Flourescent light tubes: Hazardous<br>Oil-based paint: Hazardous |
| 16.10 | A, D |
| 16.11 | B |
| 16.12 | D |
| 16.13 | B |
| 16.14 | B |
| 16.15 | C, D |
| 16.16 | A |
| 16.17 | B |
| 16.18 | C |
| 16.19 | D |
| 16.20 | C |
| 16.21 | A |

# 17 Supervisory

| | | | |
|---|---|---|---|
| 17.01 | B | 17.27 | A |
| 17.02 | B | 17.28 | D |
| 17.03 | D | 17.29 | D |
| 17.04 | A, E | 17.30 | C |
| 17.05 | C | 17.31 | B |
| 17.06 | A | 17.32 | D |
| 17.07 | B | 17.33 | B |
| 17.08 | A | 17.34 | A |
| 17.09 | B | 17.35 | A |
| 17.10 | C | 17.36 | B |
| 17.11 | D | 17.37 | B |
| 17.12 | B | 17.38 | A |
| 17.13 | B | 17.39 | B |
| 17.14 | B | 17.40 | B |
| 17.15 | C | 17.41 | D |
| 17.16 | C | 17.42 | A |
| 17.17 | C | 17.43 | C |
| 17.18 | C | 17.44 | B |
| 17.19 | B, C | 17.45 | B |
| 17.20 | B | 17.46 | D |
| 17.21 | C | 17.47 | A |
| 17.22 | B, E | 17.48 | D |
| 17.23 | A | 17.49 | C |
| 17.24 | A | 17.50 | B, D, E |
| 17.25 | B | 17.51 | D |
| 17.26 | B | 17.52 | D |

## 17 Supervisory (continued)

| | |
|---|---|
| 17.53 | C |
| 17.54 | A |
| 17.55 | D |
| 17.56 | D |
| 17.57 | 950 mm |
| 17.58 | B |
| 17.59 | 470 mm |
| 17.60 | D |
| 17.61 | A |
| 17.62 | 9 m |
| 17.63 | C |
| 17.64 | A |
| 17.65 | C |
| 17.66 | B |
| 17.67 | C |
| 17.68 | C |
| 17.69 | B |
| 17.70 | B |
| 17.71 | A |
| 17.72 | D |
| 17.73 | D |

## 18 Demolition

| | |
|---|---|
| 18.01 | B |
| 18.02 | C |
| 18.03 | A |
| 18.04 | B |
| 18.05 | C |
| 18.06 | B |
| 18.07 | 3 m |
| 18.08 | D |
| 18.09 | B |
| 18.10 | C |
| 18.11 | D |

## 18 Demolition

| | | | |
|---|---|---|---|
| 18.12 | A | 18.28 | A |
| 18.13 | B | 18.29 | B |
| 18.14 | D | 18.30 | C |
| 18.15 | B | 18.31 | C |
| 18.16 | B | 18.32 | D |
| 18.17 | D | 18.33 | D |
| 18.18 | D | 18.34 | D |
| 18.19 | A | 18.35 | B |
| 18.20 | A | 18.36 | A |
| 18.21 | B | 18.37 | D |
| 18.22 | C | 18.38 | A |
| 18.23 | B | 18.39 | D |
| 18.24 | C | 18.40 | B |
| 18.25 | C | 18.41 | C |
| 18.26 | A | 18.42 | C |
| 18.27 | B, C | | |

## 19 Highway works

| | | | |
|---|---|---|---|
| 19.01 | A | 19.08 | B |
| 19.02 | B, D | 19.09 | A |
| 19.03 | B, C | 19.10 | D |
| 19.04 | D | 19.11 | C |
| 19.05 | D | 19.12 | C |
| 19.06 | B | 19.13 | D |
| 19.07 | D | 19.14 | A |

## 19 Highway works (continued)

| | | | |
|---|---|---|---|
| 19.15 | B | 19.34 | C |
| 19.16 | C | 19.35 | D |
| 19.17 | B | 19.36 | C |
| 19.18 | B, E | 19.37 | A |
| 19.19 | C | 19.38 | B |
| 19.20 | C | 19.39 | B |
| 19.21 | A | 19.40 | A |
| 19.22 | B | 19.41 | C |
| 19.23 | C | 19.42 | C |
| 19.24 | B | 19.43 | B |
| 19.25 | A, E | 19.44 | D |
| 19.26 | C | 19.45 | B |
| 19.27 | B | 19.46 | D |
| 19.28 | B | 19.47 | D |
| 19.29 | B | 19.48 | B |
| 19.30 | D | 19.49 | D |
| 19.31 | B, E | 19.50 | B |
| 19.32 | C | 19.51 | C |
| 19.33 | A | 19.52 | A |

## 20 Specialist work at height

| | | | |
|---|---|---|---|
| 20.01 | A, C, E | 20.05 | A |
| 20.02 | B | 20.06 | C |
| 20.03 | C | 20.07 | C |
| 20.04 | C | 20.08 | D |

# 20 Specialist work at height

| Question | Answer |
|---|---|
| 20.09 | 470 mm |
| 20.10 | D |
| 20.11 | B |
| 20.12 | C |
| 20.13 | B |
| 20.14 | C |
| 20.15 | A |
| 20.16 | C |
| 20.17 | C |
| 20.18 | C, D |
| 20.19 | B |
| 20.20 | C |
| 20.21 | C |
| 20.22 | A |
| 20.23 | C |
| 20.24 | B |
| 20.25 | D |
| 20.26 | D |
| 20.27 | B |
| 20.28 | C |
| 20.29 | D |
| 20.30 | C |
| 20.31 | B |
| 20.32 | B |
| 20.33 | B, D, E |
| 20.34 | D |
| 20.35 | C, E |
| 20.36 | A |
| 20.37 | A |
| 20.38 | D |
| 20.39 | B |
| 20.40 | B |
| 20.41 | C |
| 20.42 | D |
| 20.43 | A |
| 20.44 | C |
| 20.45 | C |
| 20.46 | D |
| 20.47 | D |

## 21 Lifts and escalators

| | | | |
|---|---|---|---|
| 21.01 | B | 21.26 | A |
| 21.02 | D | 21.27 | C |
| 21.03 | A | 21.28 | C |
| 21.04 | D | 21.29 | D |
| 21.05 | A | 21.30 | A |
| 21.06 | B | 21.31 | B |
| 21.07 | C | 21.32 | A |
| 21.08 | D | 21.33 | B |
| 21.09 | B | 21.34 | A |
| 21.10 | A | 21.35 | A |
| 21.11 | B | 21.36 | C |
| 21.12 | B | 21.37 | B |
| 21.13 | C | 21.38 | A |
| 21.14 | C | 21.39 | C |
| 21.15 | A | 21.40 | B |
| 21.16 | B | 21.41 | A |
| 21.17 | B | 21.42 | C |
| 21.18 | B | 21.43 | B |
| 21.19 | C | 21.44 | D |
| 21.20 | B | 21.45 | B |
| 21.21 | A | 21.46 | A |
| 21.22 | C | 21.47 | D |
| 21.23 | A, C | 21.48 | A |
| 21.24 | A | 21.49 | A |
| 21.25 | B | | |

## 22 Tunnelling

| | |
|---|---|
| 22.01 | B |
| 22.02 | C |
| 22.03 | B |
| 22.04 | C, E |
| 22.05 | C |
| 22.06 | D |
| 22.07 | C |
| 22.08 | D |
| 22.09 | C |
| 22.10 | B |
| 22.11 | B, E |
| 22.12 | B |
| 22.13 | D |
| 22.14 | B |
| 22.15 | B |
| 22.16 | D |
| 22.17 | D |
| 22.18 | A |
| 22.19 | D |
| 22.20 | D |
| 22.21 | B |
| 22.22 | D |
| 22.23 | A |
| 22.24 | B |
| 22.25 | A |
| 22.26 | A, B |
| 22.27 | A, B |
| 22.28 | A |
| 22.29 | A |
| 22.30 | C |
| 22.31 | A |
| 22.32 | A |
| 22.33 | D |
| 22.34 | A |
| 22.35 | B, E |
| 22.36 | B |
| 22.37 | B |
| 22.38 | C |
| 22.39 | 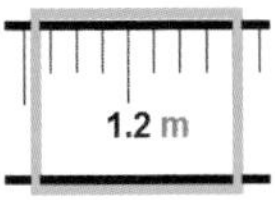 1.2 m<br>1.2 m |
| 22.40 | D |
| 22.41 | B |
| 22.42 | A |
| 22.43 | C |
| 22.44 | D |

# 23 HVACR – Heating and plumbing services

| | |
|---|---|
| 23.01 | D |
| 23.02 | C |
| 23.03 | D |
| 23.04 | D |
| 23.05 | C |
| 23.06 | A |
| 23.07 | B |
| 23.08 | A |
| 23.09 | A |
| 23.10 | A |
| 23.11 | B |
| 23.12 | D |
| 23.13 | A |
| 23.14 | B |
| 23.15 | B |
| 23.16 | D |
| 23.17 | C |
| 23.18 | B |
| 23.19 | D |
| 23.20 | C |
| 23.21 | A |
| 23.22 | B |
| 23.23 | A |
| 23.24 | C |
| 23.25 | B |
| 23.26 | A |
| 23.27 | B |
| 23.28 | D |
| 23.29 | B |
| 23.30 | D |
| 23.31 | D |
| 23.32 | A |
| 23.33 | C |
| 23.34 | A |
| 23.35 | B |
| 23.36 | C |
| 23.37 | C |
| 23.38 | A |
| 23.39 | A |
| 23.40 | D |
| 23.41 | D |
| 23.42 | B |
| 23.43 | C |
| 23.44 | B |
| 23.45 | B |

# 24 HVACR – Pipefitting and welding

| | | | |
|---|---|---|---|
| 24.01 | C | 24.25 | B |
| 24.02 | C | 24.26 | A |
| 24.03 | B | 24.27 | D |
| 24.04 | D | 24.28 | D |
| 24.05 | D | 24.29 | C |
| 24.06 | C | 24.30 | B |
| 24.07 | A | 24.31 | B |
| 24.08 | B | 24.32 | A, E |
| 24.09 | A | 24.33 | B |
| 24.10 | D | 24.34 | A |
| 24.11 | A | 24.35 | D |
| 24.12 | B | 24.36 | B |
| 24.13 | B | 24.37 | B, D |
| 24.14 | C | 24.38 | C |
| 24.15 | D | 24.39 | C |
| 24.16 | A | 24.40 | A |
| 24.17 | A | 24.41 | B |
| 24.18 | D | 24.42 | C |
| 24.19 | D | 24.43 | A |
| 24.20 | B | 24.44 | A |
| 24.21 | C | 24.45 | D |
| 24.22 | C | 24.46 | C |
| 24.23 | C | 24.47 | D |
| 24.24 | B | 24.48 | B |

## 25 HVACR – Ductwork

| Question | Answer |
|---|---|
| 25.01 | C |
| 25.02 | D |
| 25.03 | D |
| 25.04 | C |
| 25.05 | A |
| 25.06 | B |
| 25.07 | A |
| 25.08 | D |
| 25.09 | A |
| 25.10 | B |
| 25.11 | B, D |
| 25.12 | C |
| 25.13 | B |
| 25.14 | A |
| 25.15 | D |
| 25.16 | C |
| 25.17 | B |
| 25.18 | D |
| 25.19 | B |
| 25.20 | C |
| 25.21 | C |
| 25.22 | B |
| 25.23 | D |
| 25.24 | D |
| 25.25 | D |
| 25.26 | C |
| 25.27 | B |
| 25.28 | A |
| 25.29 | A |
| 25.30 | D |
| 25.31 | C |
| 25.32 | A, E |
| 25.33 | B |
| 25.34 | A |
| 25.35 | B |
| 25.36 | C |
| 25.37 | C |
| 25.38 | A |
| 25.39 | A |
| 25.40 | D |
| 25.41 | D |
| 25.42 | B |
| 25.43 | B |
| 25.44 | D |
| 25.45 | C |

## 26 HVACR – Refrigeration and air conditioning

| | |
|---|---|
| 26.01 | C |
| 26.02 | A |
| 26.03 | B |
| 26.04 | A |
| 26.05 | B |
| 26.06 | C |
| 26.07 | D |
| 26.08 | C |
| 26.09 | A |
| 26.10 | B |
| 26.11 | B |
| 26.12 | D |
| 26.13 | B |
| 26.14 | D |
| 26.15 | A |
| 26.16 | B |
| 26.17 | B |
| 26.18 | A |
| 26.19 | A |
| 26.20 | D |
| 26.21 | C |
| 26.22 | D |
| 26.23 | C |
| 26.24 | C |
| 26.25 | A |
| 26.26 | B |
| 26.27 | C |
| 26.28 | B |
| 26.29 | B |
| 26.30 | D |
| 26.31 | B |
| 26.32 | C |
| 26.33 | B |
| 26.34 | B, D |
| 26.35 | B |
| 26.36 | C |
| 26.37 | A |
| 26.38 | B |
| 26.39 | C |
| 26.40 | C |
| 26.41 | A |
| 26.42 | A |
| 26.43 | D |
| 26.44 | D |
| 26.45 | C |
| 26.46 | D |

## 27 HVACR – Services and facilities maintenance

| | |
|---|---|
| 27.01 | A |
| 27.02 | D |
| 27.03 | C |
| 27.04 | B |
| 27.05 | A |
| 27.06 | A, C |
| 27.07 | A |
| 27.08 | B |
| 27.09 | A |
| 27.10 | B |
| 27.11 | C |
| 27.12 | D |
| 27.13 | B |
| 27.14 | D |
| 27.15 | B |
| 27.16 | B, E |
| 27.17 | C |
| 27.18 | D |
| 27.19 | D |
| 27.20 | B |
| 27.21 | A |
| 27.22 | A |
| 27.23 | D |
| 27.24 | B |
| 27.25 | B |
| 27.26 | A |
| 27.27 | A |
| 27.28 | A |
| 27.29 | Between 20°C and 45°C |
| 27.30 | C |
| 27.31 | D |
| 27.32 | B |
| 27.33 | C |
| 27.34 | D |
| 27.35 | B |
| 27.36 | A |
| 27.37 | A |
| 27.38 | A |
| 27.39 | A |
| 27.40 | C |
| 27.41 | A |
| 27.42 | B |
| 27.43 | A, C |
| 27.44 | A |
| 27.45 | B |
| 27.46 | B |
| 27.47 | C |

# 28 Plumbing (JIB)

| | | | |
|---|---|---|---|
| 28.01 | B | 28.20 | D |
| 28.02 | B | 28.21 | B |
| 28.03 | B | 28.22 | B |
| 28.04 | B | 28.23 | B |
| 28.05 | A | 28.24 | C |
| 28.06 | D | 28.25 | D |
| 28.07 | C | 28.26 | A |
| 28.08 | D | 28.27 | A |
| 28.09 | B | 28.28 | B |
| 28.10 | C | 28.29 | C |
| 28.11 | A | 28.30 | D |
| 28.12 | A | 28.31 | C |
| 28.13 | D | 28.32 | A |
| 28.14 | D | 28.33 | C |
| 28.15 | B | 28.34 | D |
| 28.16 | C | 28.35 | D |
| 28.17 | A | 28.36 | B |
| 28.18 | A | 28.37 | B |
| 28.19 | B | 28.38 | D |

# Preparing for the case studies

Construction is an exciting industry. There is constant change as work progresses to completion.

As a result, the construction site is one of the most dangerous environments to work in.

Everyone on site working together can avoid many of the accidents that happen. The free film *Setting out* shows what you and the site must do to stay healthy and safe at work.

To watch the film:

 go online at *www.citb.co.uk/settingout*

This film is essential viewing for everyone involved in construction, and should be viewed before sitting the CITB *Health, safety and environment test.*

The content of the film is summarised here. These principles form the basis for the behavioural case studies.

*It is advisable to watch the film. However, for those unable to view it or who want to refresh themselves on the content, the full transcript is provided for your information.*

## Part 1: What you should expect from the construction industry

Your site and your employer should be doing all they can to keep you and your colleagues safe.

Before any work begins, the site management team will have been planning and preparing the site for your arrival. It's their job to ensure that you can do your job safely and efficiently.

**Five things the site you are working on must do:**

- ☑ know when you are on site
- ☑ give you a site induction
- ☑ give you site-specific information
- ☑ encourage communication
- ☑ keep you up to date and informed.

## Part 2: What the industry expects of you

Once the work begins, it's up to every individual to take responsibility for carrying out the plan safely.

This means you should follow the rules and guidelines as well as being alert to the continuing changes on site.

**Five things you must do:**

- ☑ respect and follow the site rules
- ☑ safely prepare each task
- ☑ carry out each task responsibly and know when to stop (if you think anything is unsafe)
- ☑ keep learning.

# Setting out – the transcript

### What to expect from the industry and what the industry expects from you

Construction is an exciting industry. There is constant change as work progresses to completion.

As a result, the construction site is one of the most dangerous environments to work in.

Many accidents that occur on sites can be avoided. In this film you will find out what you and the site must do to stay healthy and safe at work.

## Part 1: What to expect from the industry

When you arrive for your first day on a site, it will not be the first day for everyone.

Before any work begins, the site management team will have been planning and preparing the site for your arrival.

It is *their* job to ensure that you can do your job safely and efficiently.

So what are five key things the site should do for you?

### 1. Your site must know when you are on site

When you arrive you should be greeted and welcomed by someone on site. If you are not then make your presence known to site management.

You need to know who is in charge and they need to know who is working on, or visiting, their site.

You may be asked to sign in or report to someone in charge when you arrive. You should also let someone know, or sign out, if you are leaving.

### 2. Your site must give you an induction

Once you have introduced yourself, you will be given a site induction. This is a legal requirement to give you basic information so that you can work safely on site.

You may be asked to watch a video or look at a presentation. It is important that you understand what is said during the induction. If there is something you are not sure about, don't be afraid to ask for more information. If you have not been to the site for a while, you need to be sure that you are up to date. Check with site management whether you need a briefing or a further induction.

### 3. Your site must give you site-specific information

Whether you are just starting out or have decades of experience, every job is different. So it is very important that the site induction is specific to your site.

You should be told about any specific areas of danger and what site rules are in place to control these.

You will be told who the managers are on site and what arrangements are in place for emergencies.

You will also find out what to do it there is a fire or if you need to sound an alarm.

It may sound basic, but there must be good welfare facilities.

You must also be able to take a break somewhere that is warm and dry.

**4. Your site must encourage communication**
Evidence shows that there are fewer incidents and accidents on sites where workers are actively involved in health and safety. Your opinions and ideas are important so make them heard.

Whatever the size of your site there should be many opportunities to do this. For example, directly with managers through a daily briefing or through suggestion boxes. Managers should let you know how best to do this on your site.

**5. Your site must keep you up to date**
Construction sites are constantly changing and unplanned activities can be a major cause of accidents. The more up to date you are about what is happening on site, the more you can understand the dangers. The best sites keep their people informed on daily activities.

Is there a hazards board on your site – is it regularly updated?

Your site management must be telling you what's going on, on a regular basis.

**Your site should be doing all it can to keep you and your colleagues safe. If it is not – say something and work together to make it better.**

## Part 2: What the industry expects from you

Site management will have planned ahead to make work on site as safe as possible for you. Once the work begins, it is up to every individual to take responsibility for carrying out the plan safely. This means following the guidelines set out and being alert to the continuing changes on site.

So what will the site expect from you?

**1. You must respect site rules**
Site rules are there to minimise the risk of particularly hazardous activities, such as moving vehicles and handling flammable substances.

Moving traffic on site is a major cause of accidents. Often rules will cover issues like walking through the site, where to park, and how to behave when you see a moving vehicle.

They may also tell you where you can smoke and remind you to tidy equipment away when it is not in use.

These might feel restrictive but they have been put in place for a reason. If that reason is not clear to you, ask for more information. Otherwise, follow the rules to stay safe.

**2. You must safely prepare each task**
Every task carried out on site is unique and will have its own dangers, for instance working at height or manual handling. The site management team will put in place a plan to avoid or minimise the dangers before the start of work. The plan may be written down in a risk assessment, a method statement or a task sheet.

This will tell you what to do, the skills needed, what to wear, what tools to use and what the dangers are.

You should contribute to the planning process using your experience and knowledge.

For example, before working at height, which is a high-risk activity, you must consider:

☑ Is the access suitable for what you need to do?

☑ Do you have the right tools?

☑ Do you have the right protective equipment, does it fit, and is it comfortable?

**3. You must do each task responsibly**

Once you are at work you must apply your training, skills and common sense to your tasks at all times.

For example, if you are building a wall, you may have to move heavy loads. But you must not put your health and body in danger. Make sure you move the load as safely as possible, as you should have been trained to do. And if you are not sure how to, then you must ask for advice.

Equally, it is important to be aware of the dangers to those around you. For example, if someone working with you is not wearing the correct PPE for a certain activity, tell them so.

Acting responsibly will benefit both you and your colleagues.

**4. You must know when to stop**

In our industry saying NO is not easy. We are fixers and doers. We CAN do.

However, a significant number of accidents on sites happen when people are doing things that they're not comfortable with.

For example, many workers have been harmed by not knowing how to identify asbestos. If you think there is any likelihood that there is asbestos present where you are working, you must stop work and seek advice.

If you are not properly trained, equipped, or briefed – or if the situation around you changes – the result could be an accident.

Trust your instincts. If things feel beyond your control or dangerous, or if you see someone else working unsafely, stop the work immediately and inform site management why you have done so.

You might prevent an injury or save a life. Your employer should be supportive if you do this because you have the right to say no and the responsibility to not walk by.

**5. You must keep learning**

If your job requires you to have specific training to enable you to do it safely then it is your employer's responsibility to provide it.

To really get the best out of your career, you should keep learning about developments in machinery, equipment, regulations and training.

This will not only give you greater confidence and understanding, it will ensure you remain healthy and safe.

**In summary**

Construction is so much more than bricks and mortar. The work we do improves the world around us. It's time for us to work together to build a safer and better industry.

Notes

Notes

Notes

Notes

Notes